The Mechanics of Law Firm Profitability:

People, Process, and Technology

EDITED BY EDWARD BOWES

Head of events and books
Leah Darbyshire

Commissioning editor
Laura Slater

Editorial assistant
Edward Bowes

Published by ARK Group:

UK, Europe and Asia office
6–14 Underwood Street
London, N1 7JQ
United Kingdom
Tel: +44(0) 207 566 5792
publishing@ark-group.com

North America office
4408 N. Rockwood Drive, Suite 150
Peoria IL 61614
United States
Tel: +1 (309) 495 2853
publishingna@ark-group.com

www.ark-group.com

Layout by Susie Bell, www.f-12.co.uk

Printed by Canon (UK) Ltd, Cockshot Hill, Reigate, RH2 8BF, United Kingdom

ISBN: 978-1-78358-260-0

A catalogue record for this book is available from the British Library

ARK Group is a division of Wilmington plc. The company is registered in England & Wales with company number 2931372 GB
Registered office: 6-14 Underwood Street, London N1 7JQ. VAT Number: GB 899 3725 51.

Contents

Executive summary

For the majority of law firms these days there is an internal struggle between longstanding cultural norms and an evolving data-focused business environment, in which firms must be willing to adapt and accept new ways of analyzing their business. Today's hyper-competitive market requires firms to acknowledge and focus on their bottom line, and the impact their standard practices have on it.

Take the example of law firm partner compensation plans. Despite increasing client demands for AFAs, fixed fees, and a renewed emphasis on collaboration and cross-selling, compensation plans simply have not kept pace with the changing legal landscape. Rather they continue to reward yesterday's one-dimensional behaviors. For the most part law firms have yet to actually define their bottom-line, with even the determination of profit margins a relatively new measurement in the industry. This begs the question, how should the modern firm reposition itself to face these challenges?

Many law firms today are wrongly focused on increasing market share, when they should really be paying more attention to what makes them a more profitable business. Market share is irrelevant if you are not profitable. Law firms cannot simply grow their way to prosperity by way of slashing fees to undercut the competition – instead, firms must focus on value creation and increasing a client's willingness to pay for a particular service. The question should be: "What can your firm do better, or more efficiently, and more profitably than anyone else?"

The Mechanics of Law Firm Profitability: People, Process, and Technology is illustrative of the changing scope of matter management in support of client value, practice efficiency, and ultimately law firm profitability. The book examines why a focus on profitability and metrics is reshaping law firm operations and matter management; how to define the bottom line and to distinguish between "good" revenue and "bad"; and how to change the dialogue from "hours and revenue" to "revenue and profit", while changing the mindset from increasing market share to simply running a profitable business.

Keith Maziarek succinctly remarks in chapter two; "…at the end of the day, every venture is in business to bring in more money than it spends" – and law firms are no exception.

In chapter one Jack Bostelman, president of KM/JD Consulting LLC, and Chris Boyd, senior director of professional services at Wilson Sonsini Goodrich & Rosati LLP, outline how implementing knowledge management projects into a firm can increase profitability, and create more value from work undertaken. Using a base case model that is given to the reader, they show how a firm's financial figures can be improved with three kinds of Knowledge Management (KM) project – proving that a rethink of a lawyer's day-to-day practice can have tangible financial benefits.

Chapter two features Keith Maziarek, senior director of client value at Perkins Coie, outlining the weaknesses of using realization figures as the primary method of measuring profitability – and how any focus that is "revenue driven" will lead to sub-optimal business decisions. The chapter then moves on to briefly discuss the relationship between revenue and profits per partner (PPP), and how PPP can affect, and be affected by, the overall profitability of a firm.

Continuing the discussion on PPP, in chapter three Toby Brown, chief practice manager officer at Perkins Coie, explores the issue of how firms should treat partner compensation in relation to profitability – and runs through developing a comprehensive partner compensation system based on "revenue and profit" as opposed to the more current "hours and revenue" basis.

To further develop on the issue of partner compensation in terms of profitability, chapter four features Timothy Corcoran, principal of Corcoran Consulting Group LLC, discussing the complexities of partner compensation; including how firms should measure and reward profitability; keeping compensation plans transparent; and making compensation plans work during partner successions.

In chapter five Anthony Davis and Wendy Chang, partners at Hinshaw & Culbertson LLP, follow on from chapter two's considerations on "bad revenue", and how firms are moving away from the "any work is profit" mentality, to explore how a firm can use the client intake process to boost profitability. The chapter brings light to the fact that with proper client management, and the confidence to reject those clients destined to be unprofitable, a firm can make significant improvements to its profits.

Chapter six moves to focus the issue of profitability in relation to the hiring of laterals, with David Parnell, founder and principal of True

North Partner Management, discussing the upfront financial analysis of the acquisition and the nuances surrounding the first year profitability during the process.

In chapter seven, Michael Roster, co-chair of the Association of Corporate Counsel's Value Challenge Steering Committee, outlines how firms should take to viewing their different practice groups as individual, autonomous entities – and redefine the firm itself as a provider of multiple specialist services through the use of "departments" (practice groups) rather than a singular business entity. The chapter leads into explaining how some practice groups can widely differ, and judging them all by the same standards can lead to negative financial impacts. With profitability managed at an individual practice group level a firm can optimize their profits to a finer degree.

However, managing profitability is not an easy task; as Jim Hassett, founder of LegalBizDev, discusses in chapter eight. Through multiple interviews with many senior level partners at law firms, a telling picture is painted showing the obstacles that law firms face in managing their profitability – and where many of them fail. These issues often preventing firms from moving towards a position of profit include effectively controlling the bidding processes and knowing where to count a loss as "acceptable".

In chapter nine James G. Perkins, chief operating officer and chief compliance officer at Procopio, gives an overview of how the regional firm uses and manages their profitability, how they established and utilize their profitability model, and why the concept of "managing on the edge" is fundamental to firms operating at regional levels.

Finally, the book finishes with a case study from Faegre Baker Daniels which outlines how the firm managed to lay the foundations for sustainable and profitable growth within a niche market by making changes to their core practices and the overall culture of the firm. The case study gives an insider look at a number of methods Faegre Baker Daniels utilized to encourage profitability, including pricing initiatives, process improvement, and knowledge and project management.

About the authors

Jack Bostelman is president of KM/JD Consulting LLC in San Francisco, California, which advises law firm leaders on practice management, including knowledge management and other productivity improvements. Before founding KM/JD Consulting, Jack was a partner for over 20 years at pre-eminent AmLaw 20 firm Sullivan & Cromwell in New York City, where he had a nationally recognized transactional securities law practice and exercised management responsibilities.

Chris Boyd is senior director of professional services at Wilson Sonsini Goodrich & Rosati LLP in Palo Alto, California. Chris runs the firm's recruiting, training, and knowledge management programs, all of which are designed to help the firm deliver superlative value to its clients. Chris was previously an attorney at the firm and also led KM programs at several internet start-ups.

Toby Brown is chief practice management officer at Perkins Coie. In this role Toby leads the firm's revenue management and efficiency programs, legal project management, pricing, process improvement, practice innovation, alternative staffing, and new partner integration. Toby has more than a decade of experience in practice management and pricing with Am Law firms and is the former director of the Utah State Bar.

Toby presents nationally on legal pricing, marketing, technology and law firm management for associations, law firms, legal departments, law schools, and paralegal programs. He has published numerous articles on these topics, as well as a report on Law Firm Pricing: Strategies, Roles, and Responsibilities (Ark Group, 2013). He has served on a number of legal services boards, bar association task forces, and legal market organizations. He received the Peer Excellence Award, the President's Award, and the Anne Charles Award from the National Association of Bar Executives. Toby maintains the ABA award winning 3 Geeks and a Law Blog with two colleagues at: www.geeklawblog.com.

Wendy Chang, partner at Hinshaw & Culbertson, represents lawyers in all types of complex matters that involve the practice of the law, including risk management counseling, ethics, crises management, fee related issues, discipline defense, hotline counseling, professional liability, and litigation defense. Ms. Chang is a certified specialist in Legal Malpractice Law by the State Bar of California's Board of Legal Specialization. Ms. Chang is a member of the American Bar Association's Standing Committee on Ethics and Professional Responsibility, and is an advisor to the State Bar of California's Commission for the Revision of the Rules of Professional Conduct. She is a past chair of the State Bar of California's Standing Committee on Professional Responsibility and Conduct.

Ms. Chang also represents businesses in all types of business litigation, with particular emphasis in high exposure complex litigation, trials, and appeals. Ms. Chang represents corporate and governmental entities in a variety of high exposure media interest litigation, including complex tort defense, fraud and conspiracy claims, insurance litigation (coverage litigation, bad faith), contracts, and complex business disputes from filing through mediation, trial, arbitration, and/or appeal. She regularly appears before the trial courts and the courts of appeal. Ms. Chang also represents businesses in defense of employment litigation, in discrimination, harassment, and retaliation claims. She has served as an independent workplace investigator for public entities in sensitive matters relating to human resource issues.

Timothy B. Corcoran is principal of Corcoran Consulting Group, LLC, and was the 2014 president of the Legal Marketing Association. A former CEO, he specializes in helping law firm and law department leaders adapt and profit during a time of great change. He authors Corcoran's Business of Law blog and can be reached at +1.609.557.7311 and tim@corcoranconsultinggroup.com.

Anthony Davis is best described as a lawyer's lawyer. Mr. Davis is a member of the Lawyers for the Profession® practice group and his practice focuses on the laws that govern lawyers. He advises attorneys and law firms on legal professional and ethics issues, law firm creation, merger and dissolution, risk management, and loss control. Mr. Davis is a lecturer-in-law at the Columbia University School of Law, teaching "Professional Responsibility Issues in Business Practice." As an adjunct professor of law, Mr. Davis taught "Legal Profession" at Brooklyn Law School for many years. Mr. Davis has served as a member of the New

York City Bar Professional Ethics Committee and is a former chair of the Professional Development Committee.

Jim Hassett is the founder of LegalBizDev, which helps law firms increase profitability by improving project management, business development, and alternative fees. Before he started working with lawyers, Jim had 20 years of experience as a sales trainer and consultant to companies from American Express to Zurich Financial Services. He is the author of 13 books, including the *Legal Project Management Quick Reference Guide*; *Legal Project Management, Pricing, and Alternative Fee Arrangements*; *Client Value and Law Firm Profitability*; and the *Legal Business Development Quick Reference Guide*. He has also published more than 80 articles in the *New York Times Magazine*; *Bloomberg Law*; *Of Counsel*; *Legal Management*; *Strategies: The Journal of Legal Marketing*; and other publications. Jim is a frequent speaker at law firms and at bar associations (including the New York City Bar, the New York State Bar, and the Massachusetts Bar), Harvard Law School; the Association of Corporate Counsel; the Defense Research Institute; the Ark Group; and at Legal Marketing Association meetings in Boston, New York, Philadelphia, Washington, Savannah, and Vancouver. He has conducted webinars through the Ark Group; West LegalEdcenter; the National Law Journal; The International Lawyers Network; TAG Academy; and the Legal Marketing Association. Jim writes the blog "Legal Business Development" which was featured at the ABA TECHSHOW (in its list of "60 Sites: Latest and Greatest Internet Hits") and by TechnoLawyer (in its list of "the most influential legal blogs" in BlawgWorld). He received his Ph.D. in psychology from Harvard University.

Keith Maziarek recently joined Perkins Coie as the senior director of client value. In this newly-created role, Keith works closely with the legal operations executives at the firm's top clients to establish strategic pricing arrangements, implement customized communication/collaboration tools and efficiency solutions, improve performance monitoring and reporting, optimize service delivery models, and establish metrics that will enable client legal departments to qualify and quantify the value they are capturing through their work with the firm.

Prior to joining Perkins Coie, Keith served as Head of Strategic Pricing for DLA Piper LLP. There he developed, implemented, and managed the firm's strategic pricing, profitability, and legal project management functions, with a focus on the practice in the Americas.

Keith has authored several published articles on the topic of alternative fee arrangements, and also speaks regularly at industry conferences. He is the immediate past co-chair of the LMA's annual P3 Conference, the industry's largest annual event addressing transformation in the legal industry related to pricing, project management, and process improvement. Keith holds an M.B.A. from the Kellogg School of Management at Northwestern University, with majors in Management and Strategy, Managerial Economics, and Analytical Consulting, and a B.S. in Business Management from the University of Illinois-Chicago.

David J. Parnell is an author, speaker, *Forbes* and *American Lawyer Media* columnist, and the founder and principal of True North Partner Management, a partner-level legal search and placement firm. Along with his experience in private placement, he has previously worked in-house with the likes of Intel, Xircom, and DreamWorks SKG. Complementing his *Forbes* and *ALM* columns, his work can also be found in publications such as *The American Lawyer*, *Huffington Post*, *Venture Capital Post*, *Fox News Magazine*, *Lawyerist*, *Law360*, *Bloomberg*, *Australasian Lawyer*, *NBC News*, *The Global Legal Post*, *Business Insider*, and *NZ Lawyer*, among others.

James G. Perkins, chief operating officer and chief compliance officer at Procopio, leads the firm's non-legal operations including finance, human resources, administration, marketing, and information services. With 20 years of experience at the firm, he has more than 35 years total leading as a chief operating and chief financial officer in the professional services, management consulting and manufacturing industries.

Steven Petrie manages the strategy and operations department at Faegre Baker Daniels. In this capacity, he oversees the collection, extraction, and application of financial data and performance metrics for purposes of business analysis, practice development, creative pricing, and strategic planning. Steve holds a Yellow Belt certification in Legal Lean Sigma and provides guidance for the firm's institutional efforts in the areas of legal process improvement and project management. Steve's department is also home to the firm's administrative operation functions. Prior to his career in law firm management, Steve worked for the strategy and operations practice of a large consulting firm. He is a frequent industry contributor on topics of law firm economics, profitability analysis, alternative pricing, and process efficiency.

Michael Roster is co-chair of the Association of Corporate Counsel's Value Challenge Steering Committee. He was formerly managing partner of Morrison & Foerster's Los Angeles office as well as co-chair of the firm's Financial Services Practice Group worldwide, resident in both Los Angeles and Washington, DC.

Mike was subsequently general counsel of Stanford University, Stanford Medical Center, and Stanford Management Company – and then executive vice president and general counsel of Golden West Financial Corporation. He has also served as an outside director and vice chair of Silicon Valley Bank, chair of the Stanford Alumni Association, chair of the Association of Corporate Counsel, and chair of two start-up companies (Insert Therapeutics and Encirq). He is a former director of the California Bankers Association and the Federal Home Loan Bank of San Francisco.

Mike is currently an adjunct faculty member at USC Gould School of Law where he teaches advanced contracts. He also is a director of MDRC, a non-profit corporation based in New York that evaluates the effectiveness of government and other non-profit programs, and several years ago he chaired a project funded by two foundations that developed a private sector approach to eliminate abuses in consumer credit cards in the US.

Vanessa Savoie is a senior strategy and pricing analyst at Faegre Baker Daniels law firm in Minneapolis. She is part of a team that works with firm leadership to provide data driven solutions so that attorneys may best serve their clients, and effectively manage their practices. In support of firm management, she applies analytical rigor with creative problem solving to the business review process, complex financial modeling, pricing, and strategic planning. She truly enjoys partnering with and supporting the firm's professionals across the country and internationally.

Vanessa studied Psychology and graduated with honors from the University of Wisconsin-Stout in 1996. After graduation she transitioned her interest in research design, methodology, and statistics into a career in Finance and Technology. She has been fortunate to have worked at some of the Twin Cities' largest companies, including; U.S. Bank, Carlson Companies, FICO, and Ameriprise Financial.

In her spare time, she loves spending time on the run with her two children, dog, and horse. Vanessa has also recently discovered obstacle races, enjoys the challenge of training for them, and likes competing in them with friends.

Tom Snavely has almost two decades of process improvement, operations management, and project management experience. He earned an M.S. in Technology Management from the University of St. Thomas, a Certified Black Belt in Lean Six Sigma, and a Mini Master of the Lean Enterprise. Tom has developed Lean Six Sigma programs and training for several organizations that were new to these concepts. He has created and developed project management offices for several organizations to align project opportunities to strategic goals and the ultimate success of these projects. As a consultant and an operations manager, Tom has aided several organizations, and a private equity firm, to achieve strategic operational goals through process improvement and organizational change management. As a project manager, Tom has led operational and information technology projects for new innovative applications and complex business systems such as PeopleSoft and SAP. Tom has co-authored an article that is based on developing teamwork as a method to foster innovation, an article focused on collaboration with clients to optimize law firm operations for *Managing Partner*, and a chapter for an Ark publication that shares how Faegre Baker Daniels has implemented process improvement and legal project management. He has helped a local university develop a curriculum that is designed to teach MBA students Lean Six Sigma and its applications in the "real world." Tom is involved with youth development programs throughout the twin cities and is a board member for the Minneapolis YMCA.

Mark Voigtmann is a partner at Faegre Baker Daniels and leader of the firm's construction law and real estate litigation practices. He is the author of *The Automation Legal Reference: A Guide to Legal Risk in the Automation, Robotics and Process Industries*, published by the North Carolina-based International Society of Automation. He also co-authored a set of contract documents created for an incremental, education-based lean project delivery model used in two $200 million hospital projects, among others. Both within the firm and in the construction industry, Mark implements sophisticated project management and process improvement strategies to deliver optimal efficiency across the board.

Chapter 1:
Using knowledge management to increase firm profitability and pricing predictability

by Jack Bostelman, president of KM/JD Consulting LLC, and Chris Boyd, senior director of professional services, Wilson Sonsini Goodrich & Rosati LLP

Introduction

Knowledge management (KM) can enable a firm to deliver greater value to clients by connecting each attorney to the expertise and experience of every other attorney in the firm. KM resources include work product (e.g., annotated forms, checklists, and sample documents), matter profiles, expertise locators, and many others.

This article will explain how a firm can also use KM to increase firm profitability by setting forth a base-case profitability model and then showing through three case studies how the implementation of different KM resources can affect the model's variables in ways that increase overall profitability. A reader can adjust the model's inputs – attorney headcount, associate leverage, billing rates, etc. – to reflect her or his particular situation. The article will also show how effective KM can increase pricing predictability.

The first appendix to this article contains the full financial model calculations for each of the examples discussed in the article. A second appendix outlines practical techniques for implementing KM resources.

First financial case study – Practice efficiency improvements

The first part of this discussion of practice efficiency improvements considers their effect on the firm as a whole (macro view). The second part considers their effect on an individual matter (micro view).

Macro view (entire firm)

The financial returns to a law firm from each type of KM project can be measured through the project's effect on the key financial drivers of profitability, which is the most essential financial metric for any business. The examples in this article illustrate the effects of three specific types of KM projects on these key financial drivers, and hence on law firm profitability.

Profitability is discussed as profits per partner, which allows comparisons across the different examples. "Partner" means "equity partner" unless otherwise stated. Definitions of the key financial drivers of profitability are in the sidebar. The full model calculations are included in Appendix A.

Assumptions used in the models

The examples in this article are based on the following assumptions:

- Firm size: 100 lawyers;
- Leverage: 50 partners/50 associates;
- Expense ratio: 50 percent;
- Billing rates and billable hours (utilization):
  - Partners $500/hour – 1,100 hours/year; and
  - Associates $250/hour – 1,400 hours/year.

Those assumptions result in the following revenues and profits:

- Total collected billings (revenues) = $45 million; and
- Profits per partner = $450,000.

In general, the greater the associate leverage or the higher the billing rates or annual billable hours, the greater will be the profits per partner improvements in the three examples. The size of the firm has relatively little effect on the results.

Example 1 – Practice efficiency improvements

The first example illustrates the effect of practice efficiency improvements on profitability. In this scenario, the firm seeks to reduce write-downs and write-offs by performing the same work in less time. The billable time saved would be spent working on new billable matters, in which case Utilization would not decline. If the program works:

- Realization Rate will increase.

Because in this scenario efficiency savings go straight to the firm's bottom line, the benefit can be dramatic. If 5 percent of partner hours and 10 percent of associate hours are currently not collected because of write-downs and write-offs, and the program cuts those non-collected hours in half, profits per partner will increase by 8 percent. Even if the program cuts those non-collected hours by only 10 percent, profits per partner will still increase by 2 percent.

If new billable work is not available, the decline in Utilization – in other words lawyers working fewer hours – will offset the Realization Rate improvement, resulting in no change in profits per partner. Lawyers will have more available time, however, to work on developing new business or improving their skills.

Of course, this example begs the question of what specific practice improvements are envisioned. Some examples are discussed later in this article. The point of this financial example is that an improvement in Realization Rate through efficiency gains has a powerful effect on profits per partner, and is an area in which it is worth focusing KM efforts.

It should also be noted that, whatever practice improvements are employed, some amount of billable time during the first year will need to be redirected to build the KM resources being used, and possibly some billable time will need to be redirected in future years to maintain those resources. That time investment will reduce the profitability improvements shown. If most of the investment occurs in the first year, however, the returns for *each* year in the future will be at or close to the return shown, with no further investment needed.

Micro view (individual matter)

Effective KM can not only increase the overall profitability of a firm, but also increase the profitability of specific matters. The clearest way to show this is with a fixed-fee matter, which is both topical and realistic given that the prevalence of these kinds of matters is increasing. For example, consider the following assumptions for a straightforward fixed-fee transaction:

- Fixed fee for services: $25,000;
- Average time recorded: 88 hours, comprised of:
  - Partner: 20 hours @ $500/hour = $10,000;
  - Associate: 48 hours @ $250/hour = $12,000; and
  - Paralegal: 20 hours @ $150/hour = $3,000.

Now assume the firm invests in KM resources that reduce the time required to conduct due diligence and draft deal documents by an average of five associate hours per transaction. These resources could include form documents, checklists, and perhaps even artificial intelligence tools. The firm could apply that saved time – five associate hours at $250 per hour, or $1,250 – in several ways: (a) retain it as per-matter profit, (b) pass it along to the client via a lower fixed fee, or (c) some combination of both. When multiplied by hundreds of matters (assuming that the matter type is relatively frequent), the aggregate savings to the firm, the client, or both can be substantial.

Two caveats should be noted in connection with this example:

- For the scenarios where the firm retains some or all of the savings, the per-matter profit to the firm will not increase by the full amount of the saved hours multiplied by the hourly billing rate. Rather, this profit will be discounted by both the percentage of saved hours that the firm can apply to other paying work as well as the realization rate on the re-used hours. For example, if 100 percent of the saved hours are applied to new work, and the realization rate on that work is 90 percent, then the additional profit to the firm is $1,125 and not $1,250.
- The total return to the firm of these KM investments must also be reduced by the cost of the investments, including the attorney time required to develop the resources, the licensing cost of any content or software involved in the resources, and so forth.

Drivers for professional services firms that use hourly billing

In professional services firms that bill by the hour, the following formula with five drivers explains profits per partner:

Profits per partner =

Realization rate (actual revenues ÷ standard rate revenues*) **x**

Average standard rate (standard rate revenues* ÷ # hours billed) **x**

Leverage (# timekeepers ÷ # partners) **x**

Margin (revenues - expenses, as a percent of revenues) **x**

Utilization (# hours billed ÷ # timekeepers)

This five driver model is most relevant to our discussion because, at least for now, hourly billing remains the predominant approach among Am Law 200 firms (in other words, the 200 largest US law firms by revenues, as reported annually by the American Lawyer). Timekeepers consist of partners, counsel, associates, paralegals, and certain other specialists who bill by the hour, with partners (equity and non-equity) and associates responsible for the great majority of time billed.

In business terms, these five drivers can be thought of as follows:

- Realization rate is the percentage of standard billing rates that is actually collected. It reflects agreed-upon discounts from standard rates, write-downs (fee reductions taken before sending the bill), and write-offs (fee reductions after sending the bill).
- Average standard rate represents the blended hourly rate for the firm that would have been realized if billed hours were collected at standard rates. Average standard rate times realization rate equals the firm's actual average hourly rate.

  [Average realized rate, which for brevity is used in the models in this article, is simply the product of realization rate and average standard rate.]
- Leverage is the ratio of fee-earners to equity owners – conceptually the associate/partner ratio. Mathematically, Leverage is 1 plus the associate/partner ratio.
- Margin is the traditional profit margin concept – the percentage of revenues that become profit after payment of related expenses.
- Utilization is also sometimes referred to as Productivity. It is the average number of hours billed by each timekeeper during the period being considered. For a firm that bills by the hour, the most productive timekeepers are those who work the most hours.

Success towards the KM goals of improved efficiency, improved quality, and reduced risk can be measured in terms of the five drivers. Improved efficiency could increase Realization Rate by reducing write-downs and write-offs or could increase Leverage. Improved quality could increase Realization Rate or the Average Standard Rate. Reduced risk could prevent a lower Realization Rate or Average Standard Rate, or could avoid expenses that reduce Margin.

*Standard rate revenues are the revenues that would have been earned if the hours of the various timekeepers had been billed at the firm's standard hourly rates.

Further explanation of efficiency and its benefits

Efficiency is producing what the client perceives as the same legal result in fewer hours or with lower-priced lawyers, such as:

- performing the same work more efficiently to reduce the cost to the firm;
- eliminating waste; or
- avoiding what is not needed or valued by the client.

Faster response time may also be a positive byproduct of improved efficiency, but is not the driving objective. Actions that may reduce cost or waste include:

- staffing with the lowest cost lawyers who are competent to perform the work;
- use of KM resources, templates or checklists; or
- legal process improvement.

Improved efficiency brings two important benefits: happier clients and happier lawyers. Clients are happier because they experience:

- lower legal fees for the same or even higher quality results;
- quicker turnaround; and
- less time managing outside counsel.

The firm's lawyers are happier because they experience:

- improved realization and profitability;
- better client relationships and referrals;
- efficient client teams who know the clients' industries; and
- more time for business development or a personal life.

Clearing up a financial misconception

A common misconception is that lawyers who bill by the hour have no economic incentive to become more productive or efficient. The examples discussed in this article demonstrate that assertion to be untrue. Example 1, showing the increase in profits per partner caused by reducing write-offs and write-downs, illustrates this point in a straightforward way.

Even where a firm has no write-offs or write-downs, as long as there is new work available to use up the lawyers' freed-up time, financial modeling shows that improved efficiency will not reduce profits per partner, which will remain unchanged, even as fees to clients for each matter *decline*. That is advantageous because it makes the firm more fee-competitive, enables the firm to deliver more value to clients, and increases the strength of the firm's client relationships.

Even where available new work is scarce for a firm, it is likely that other firms will be making the same kind of efficiency improvements, on the expectation that they can get new work through the lower fees resulting from efficiency. To remain competitive and avoid losing work, the firm without new work will still need to lower its fees. In the absence of efficiency improvements, the firm can lower its fees only through write-downs. As shown by Example 1, efficiency improvements will reduce those write-downs and increase the lawyer time available for seeking new business.

How KM can increase fee predictability

Clients and firms both want legal fees to be more predictable. Greater fee predictability helps clients better evaluate firms, budget for legal spending, and assess value delivered. Greater fee predictability also helps firms win and retain business, staff matters, and improve service delivery.

Effective KM can increase fee predictability in two ways. First, tracking matters and profiling them in detail, and connecting those profiles to legal fees, can help firms better predict the likely fees of any potential matter. Detailed information about past cases or deals helps a firm's pricing professionals build better budgeting and pricing models to apply to future matters. In addition, a firm's finance or KM team can provide attorneys seeking to estimate fees for a current matter with apples-to-apples fee data from similar past matters.

Secondly, KM and training resources can help a case, deal, or other matter team deliver legal services more consistently, which helps that team's actual fees come in as close as possible to the predicted fees. Regardless of whether a firm is delivering the matter on a billable-hour or fixed-fee basis, hitting the estimated or fixed number makes both the client and the firm happier. Combining the pre-work training on how to do a specific type of work with in-the-moment forms, checklists, and other resources is a particularly effective way to ensure that relatively frequent and straightforward legal work is performed both well and efficiently.

Examples of KM resources

There are many types of KM resources. A few of the more common ones are described below.

1. **Work product**. Model and precedent documents that lawyers consult for guidance, or use as starting points for drafting new deal or case documents. Work product typically comes in the format of a Microsoft Word document (for forms and other models) or scanned PDFs (for matter precedents). Some firms have automated model documents using document assembly software. Good models and precedents help lawyers draft new work product more efficiently with greater consistency and quality, thereby clients receive better work faster. Note that work product can be internal (such as briefs previously drafted by the firm) or external (such as other firms' responses to regulatory inquiries, or model forms from third-party subscription services such as Practical Law Company or Practising Law Institute). Similarly, work product can be made available to a practice group, an entire firm, the firm and select clients, or the firm and all clients.
2. **Matter experience databases**. Searchable descriptions and metadata of deals, cases, and other matters, combined with key matter documents. Lawyers can search these profiles to find matters similar to ones they are working on to see how "market" terms are evolving, to get documents from past deals that may provide good starting points for research or drafting, to estimate fees for future matters, to find who in the firm has worked on similar issues, to put together a matter experience list for a new client pitch, and so forth. Matter experience databases can also be internal (such as homegrown deal databases) or external (such as searchable interfaces compiled by vendors that aggregate publicly-filed deal and case information).
3. **Expertise locators**. Resources that enable lawyers to find an expert who knows something or someone. The expertise can be general, for example Swedish mergers and acquisitions law, or specific, such as recent experience addressing a specific Securities and Exchange Commission comment in a recent initial public offering. As above, these resources can be internal (such as an expertise-focused search engine or a proprietary law firm or witness database) or external.
4. **Training**. Group training and individual mentoring that helps the firm's lawyers do their jobs well. This includes substantive training,

such as the formal junior lawyer programs and "adult education" training given to senior associates and partners, and the informal training that occurs at practice group meetings. This formal substantive training can be internal or external. Training for KM purposes also includes formal and informal training about how to discover and use the firm's KM resources themselves. While many law firm KM leaders would not consider training to be part of KM, others would, and we have included it here to show the returns to initiatives that blend KM and training.

There are many other types of KM resources. These include holding effective practice group meetings, creating a culture of sharing information and ready collaboration, checklists describing steps to complete a matter or parts of a matter (aka playbooks), annotated checklists in lieu of standard forms, and specialized software such as products designed to summarize contract terms or analyze the range of variations of certain types of provisions across a collection of contracts of the same type.

While these kinds of KM resources are traditionally thought of as investments in the quality of work product and client service, they can and should also be used to increase firm profitability and pricing predictability. The next sections of this article will outline two more financial examples showing how investment in a KM initiative can increase firm profitability.

Second financial case study – shift work from partners to associates

The second financial case study involves a KM initiative with a more complicated effect on the key drivers of profitability.

By developing KM tools and rolling them out with targeted associate training, the firm seeks to shift some of its work from partners to associates, in effect moving the associates up the work food chain and providing more value to clients by delivering work of equivalent quality at a lower price. For example, a firm's patent litigation practice might spot an opportunity to take on more defense cases against non-practicing entities by delegating much of the work traditionally done by partners to associates. To do this, the firm invests in the development of pre-approved templates for standard case documents, checklists and other matter management tools to help keep the cases on track, and detailed training for associates on how to use them to achieve good results quickly for clients.

This initiative, if successful, will require hiring more associates to handle the greater workload. The goal is that partners use most of their new "free" time to take on new work on the same basis (in terms of the five profitability drivers) as existing work. Servicing that new work will also require hiring additional associates. Some of the partners' new "free" time will also need to be spent training associates, and some of the associates' time will need to be spent attending training. If this program works:

- Leverage will increase because of the additional associates;
- Average Standard Rate will decline because associates are billed at lower hourly rates than partners;
- Utilization will increase because there will be more associates (who generally work longer hours) in the mix; and
- Possibly, Realization Rate will increase because partners may be willing more fully to bill and clients more fully to pay the lower fees resulting from a greater associate mix.

The goal is that the decreases in Average Standard Rate will be more than offset by improvements in the other drivers, resulting in higher profits per partner – notably, while also reducing the cost to clients of the work! Using the assumptions previously noted regarding partner/associate mix, billing and realization rates, margin and annual hours billed, *if*:

- half the partners shift one billable hour per week to preparing the KM tools and conducting the training;
- all the associates shift one billable hour every other week to learning how to use the KM tools and attending training;
- the tools and training result in associates taking on 15 percent of partner work at the rate of 1.5 hours of associate time per partner hour assumed (on the theory that the associates, even with tools and training, cannot complete the work as fast as the partners);
- saved partner time is devoted to new fee-paying work; and
- more associates are hired to help partners on the new work,

then profits per partner will *increase* 5.3 percent (even with no improvement in Realization Rate) and clients will see a 4.1 percent fee *reduction*.

Example 2 assumes more billable work is available. If it is not, profits per partner decline marginally, and partners have more time to work on developing new business – which, all else being equal, may be more likely to be obtained given the increased value the firm is delivering to its clients and their increased satisfaction level. This and other consequences of new work not being available have been discussed above under "Clearing up a financial misconception."

Third financial case study – more efficient partner pitch preparation

The third example illustrates another situation in which a KM initiative affects multiple financial drivers and has the net effect of increasing profits per partner.

Through improved data collection about matters, the firm seeks to save partner time in preparing and revising pitch materials, allowing the partners to apply that saved time to billable work. (Again, Example 3 assumes more billable work is available. If it is not, the project may improve the partners' quality of life but would not improve profits.) For example, the firm establishes a deal database for its transactional matters with sufficient detail to allow the marketing department to quickly and accurately show experience with specific kinds of transactions in specific industries, and a similar litigation case database containing experience with specific legal issues in specific jurisdictions (or even with specific judges). These databases are intended to eliminate the time spent by partners contacting their colleagues for this information.

If the program works:

- Utilization will increase because partners are billing more hours; and
- Average Standard Rate will increase slightly because of the greater number of partner hours in the mix.

Using the same law firm assumptions as the previous examples, if half the partners save two billable hours per week, profits per partner will increase about 6 percent (assuming no change in annual expenses).

Somewhat surprisingly, the cost of the new data collection system does not affect the outcome very much. For a 100-lawyer firm, a one-time $200,000 cost would reduce the profits per partner benefit by only 1 percent in the first year (to 5 percent), with no reduction in future years. Profit improvement is fairly linear to the time saved by partners. If half the partners save only one-quarter of a billable hour per week, profits per partner improve only 0.3 percent, which in practical terms is probably the break-even point for this initiative.

Investment of billable time to create the database will reduce the first-year benefit somewhat. Any ongoing billable time required to maintain the database in future years will also reduce the benefit a bit in those years. These time investments should be estimated and modeled before the initiative is undertaken. In addition, there may be other efficiency benefits of the initiative that should be modeled, such as using the database to more quickly identify similar matters for purposes of finding example documents.

Conclusion

This article has sought to demonstrate that changes to the way lawyers practice can have real financial benefits to both firms and clients. Any project can be analyzed under the law firm financial model. Of course, possible benefits used as model inputs are inherently judgment calls. One way to view the analysis of the model is as a way to discover the break-even point for benefits. After determining the assumptions that lead to the break-even point, ask yourself and your colleagues whether they believe that level of benefit is achievable. If there is reasonable confidence the break-even level will be achieved, then it makes sense to proceed with the initiative.

Appendix A – The three financial models

Base Case – Financial model for hourly billing

	Average annual billable hours	Average annual written-off hours	Average annual non-billable admin hours	Billing rate	# in firm
Partners	1,100	58	100	$500	50
Associates	1,400	156	50	$250	50
				Total lawyers	100

Annual expenses = $22,500,000

Average realized rate = total annual billings ÷ # hrs billed

Total billings = (1,100*$500*50) + (1,400*$250*50) =	$ 45,000,000.00
# hrs billed = (1,100*50) + (1,400*50) =	125,000
ARR =	$ 360.00

Leverage = # lawyers ÷ # partners

Leverage =	(50 + 50) ÷ 50 =	2.00

Margin = (total annual billings - expenses) ÷ total annual billings

Margin =	($45,000,000 - $22,500,000) ÷ $45,000,000 =	50 %

Utilization = total annual hours billed ÷ # lawyers

Utilization =	(1,100*50 + 1,400*50) ÷ (50+50) =	1,250

Profit Per Partner = ARR * Leverage * Margin * Utilization = $ 450,000.00

Example 1 – Practice efficiency improvements

5 percent of partner hours and 10 percent of associate hours are written off before or after the bill is sent, due to inefficiency or client fee sensitivities.

Through practice improvements, the lawyers become efficient enough that matters are completed in fewer hours.
As a result, written off hours are reduced 50 percent, with those saved hours being billed and collected on other new work.
For simplicity, the model treats all write-offs as soft, with 100 percentage of billings being collected.

	Average annual billable hours	Average annual written-off hours	Average annual non-billable admin hours	Billing rate	# in firm
Partners	1,129	29	100	$500	50
Associates	1,478	78	50	$250	50
				Total lawyers	100

Annual expenses = $22,500,000

			Base Case
Average realized rate = total annual billings ÷ # hrs billed			
Total billings = (1,129*$500*50) + (1,478*$250*50) =		$ 46,700,000.00	$ 45,000,000.00
# hrs billed = (1,129*50) + (1,478*50) =		130,350	125,000
ARR =		$ 358.27	$ 360.00
Leverage = # lawyers ÷ # partners			
Leverage =	(50 + 50) ÷ 50 =	2.00	2.00
Margin = (total annual billings - expenses) ÷ total annual billings			
Margin =	($46,700,000 - $22,500,000) ÷ $46,700,000 =	52 %	50 %
Utilization = total annual hours billed ÷ # lawyers			
Utilization =	(1,129*50 + 1,478*50) ÷ (50+50) =	1,304	1,250
Profit Per Partner = ARR * Leverage * Margin * Utilization =		$ 484,000.00	$ 450,000.00

Result: Profits per partner improve by $34,000 (8 %), or a total of $1,700,000 per year.

Example 2 – Shift work from partners to associates

Half the partners shift this many hours per week (percentage of average billable time) to training & forms:	1.00 (2.3 %)
All the associates shift this many hours per week (percentage of average billable time) to attending training:	0.50 (1.8 %)
As a result, additional associates take on this percentage of partner billable time, at the rate of 1.5 associate hours per partner hour assumed and with no added partner hours for supervision:	15 %

Partners devote their spare billable time (difference of above items) to new work, using additional associates at the same leverage.

Increase in number of associates is 18 (8.8 to handle former partner work and 8.7 for new work, rounded up).

Expenses increase at 50 percent of per associate billing rate to reflect new associate salaries and overhead.

	Average annual billable hours	Average annual written-off hours	Average annual non-billable admin hours	Billing rate	# in firm
Partners	1,075	57	125	$500	50
Associates	1,375	153	75	$250	68
				Total lawyers	118

Annual expenses = $26,550,000

			Billings for old work:
Average realized rate = total annual billings ÷ # hrs billed			
Total billings = (1,075*$500*50) + (1,375*$250*68) =		$ 50,250,000.00	$ 43,140,625.00
# hrs billed = (1,075*50) + (1,375*68) =		147,250	**Base Case**
ARR =		$ 341.26	$ 360.00
Leverage = # lawyers ÷ # partners			
Leverage =	(68 + 50) ÷ 50 =	2.36	2.00
Margin = (total annual billings - expenses) ÷ total annual billings			
Margin =	($50,250,000 - $26,550,000) ÷ $50,250,000 =	47 %	50 %
Utilization = total annual hours billed ÷ # lawyers			
Utilization =	(1,075*50 + 1,375*68) ÷ (50+68) =	1,248	1,250
Profit Per Partner = ARR * Leverage * Margin * Utilization =		$ 474,000.00	$ 450,000.00

Result: Profits per partner improve by $24,000 (5.3 %), or a total of $1,200,000 per year.
Note that ARR and margin decline slightly.
Billings to clients for old work actually decline 4.1 %.

Example 3 – More efficient partner pitch preparation

Additional annual partner billable hours per partner: 50
No increase in total annual expenses.

	Average annual billable hours	Average annual written-off hours	Average annual non-billable admin hours	Billing rate	# in firm
Partners	1,150	61	50	$500	50
Associates	1,400	156	50	$250	50
				Total lawyers	100

Annual expenses = $22,500,000

			Base Case
Average realized rate = total annual billings ÷ # hrs billed			
Total billings =	(1,150*$500*50) + (1,400*$250*50) =	$ 46,250,000.00	$ 45,000,000.00
# hrs billed =	(1,150*50) + (1,400*50) =	127,500	125,000
ARR =		$ 362.75	$ 360.00
Leverage = # lawyers ÷ # partners			
Leverage =	(50 + 50) ÷ 50 =	2.00	2.00
Margin = (total annual billings - expenses) ÷ total annual billings			
Margin =	($46,250,000 - $22,500,000) ÷ $46,250,000 =	51 %	50 %
Utilization = total annual hours billed ÷ # lawyers			
Utilization =	(1,150*50 + 1,400*50) ÷ (50+50) =	1,275	1,250
Profit Per Partner = ARR * Leverage * Margin * Utilization =		$ 475,000.00	$ 450,000.00

Result: Profits per partner improve by $25,000 (6 %), or a total of $1,250,000 per year.

Appendix B – How to start/restart a KM practice efficiency program

Select a pilot practice group

A firm that wishes to start a KM practice efficiency program, or reinvigorate its existing efforts, should pilot its effort in a single practice group. Concentrating its efforts in one group will allow greater progress to be made, enabling the firm to demonstrate the benefits of the effort to other practice groups.

It is important that the candidate practice group be one whose leaders want to improve efficiency, even if they are unsure how to accomplish that. The group should also have enough visibility within the firm, by virtue of size or reputation, that its successes will be noticed by other groups.

Although each group's particular KM needs will differ, the pilot group's success will nevertheless inspire others to try, because many of the same KM concepts will work. For example, a checklist can benefit any practice group, even though the content of the checklist will be specific to a particular group.

Hold a meeting of the group

After the pilot group is identified, a kick-off meeting of the group should be held for the purpose of brainstorming KM ideas. The lawyers should be asked to think broadly. For example, they could be asked, "What changes would make your life easier as a practicing lawyer?"

In addition to gathering ideas from those who know what can really make a difference, the meeting serves the second important purpose of gaining buy-in from the group's lawyers because they "own" the ideas. The meeting should include one to two dozen lawyers, reflecting a cross-section of seniority levels from junior associate to senior partner and office locations. As many lateral lawyers as possible should be invited as well. They bring a helpful perspective because they can describe KM initiatives that have worked at their prior firms.

The meeting can be run by a partner of the firm or by an outside facilitator. The meeting leader should keep a list of all the suggestions. Even with a broad question such as the one suggested above, almost all the ideas will likely fall in the KM area.

Prioritize the KM projects

For the same reason the firm should focus its initial efforts in a single practice group, the practice group should focus its initial efforts on a limited number of initiatives. It is likely the ideas from the meeting will exceed the group's capacity to implement them. How, then, should the group's leader decide which opportunities to pursue and which to set aside, at least for the moment?

One useful prioritization method was set forth by Oz Benamram and Sally Gonzalez in a 2011 article.[2] The practice group, assisted by the KM team, should map potential KM projects on a two-by-two matrix, with one axis being ease of implementation and the other being value to the business, as illustrated below:

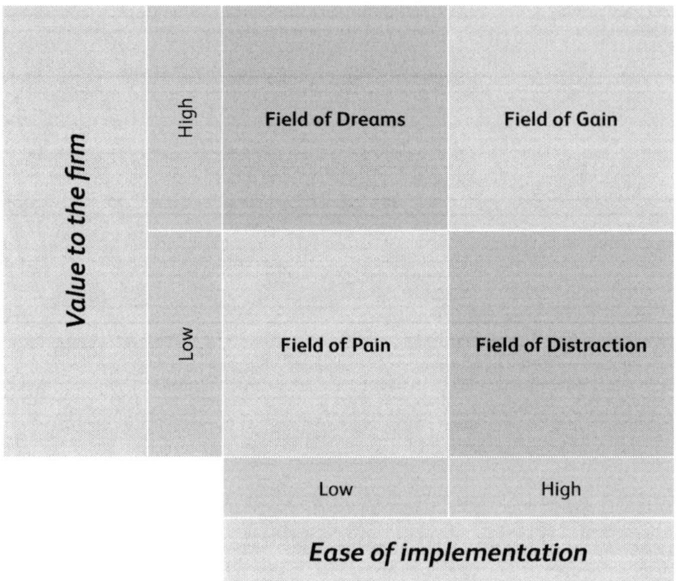

One way to accomplish that is for the practice group to assign a 1–5 rating to value (5 being highest) and ease of implementation (5 being easiest), then rank projects based on the sum of the two ratings. Values can be assigned in a variety of ways, from informally via show of hands at a meeting to more formally via detailed analyses and cost-benefit calculations. Assessing ease of implementation should take into account factors such as:

- Management and practice group support – the greater support is, the easier implementation will be.
- Number of lawyers who must cooperate – the lower the number, the easier implementation will be.

- Process feasibility – the fewer process changes required, the easier implementation will be.
- Technical feasibility – the less complex or dedicated technology required, the easier implementation will be.
- Size of investment required for both development and maintenance – the lower the investment, the easier implementation will be.

For example, checklists are typically on the easier end of the spectrum, because they can be created by a few lawyers for the benefit of many, and at least at the basic level do not require dedicated technology. Assessing value to the business should take into account factors such as:

- The potential financial returns from the project, as discussed in this article.
- The potential non-financial returns from the project, including enhancing reputation and brand (or avoiding reputational harm), improving client satisfaction and improving lawyer morale and retention.
- The number of people likely to use the resource to be developed, in other words, the target user group multiplied by the likely adoption rate. One way to assess this factor is to seek input at a meeting of 10–20 lawyers representing a cross-section of the affected practice group(s). This approach also aids in acceptance of the project by the group because they are more likely to buy in to its rationale and potential benefits.

Once the KM projects are mapped onto the matrix, the team should go for the quick wins in the Field of Gain, steadily chip away at the Field of Dreams, and avoid the Fields of Pain and Distraction.

Implement the projects

Timing and accountability

Successful execution of top-priority projects depends on effective application of traditional accountability and project management techniques. First, the practice group should assign each project to a small team and staff it like a matter. A particularly notable way to instill accountability is to make the assignments at a practice group meeting, so that the attorneys' peers see who is on which projects.

Second, the group's leader(s) should set deadlines for all projects. The ideal scope is one achievable in six months – long enough to demonstrate clear accomplishments, yet short enough to maintain the momentum of the initiative and harness lawyers' natural tendencies for urgency. A three-month check-in at project midpoint can be a useful way to provide guidance and oversight along with any necessary course corrections and resource re-assignments.

Finally, to keep each project team focused, the practice group leader(s) should require the teams to provide weekly status reports that are circulated to the entire group. This both provides peer pressure and instills healthy and productive competition among the project teams.

Other implementation considerations

It is very likely that some of the group's KM projects will involve creation of materials to which lawyers in the group will need ready access on an ongoing basis – for example, checklists or a spreadsheet containing a master matter list with profile data. As part of the overall KM pilot initiative, the group should establish a way for group members to access these materials. An ideal location would be the group's intranet site. A byproduct of using the intranet is that it may be revitalized by having this fresh content. A shared drive or folder in the document management system could also be used, although those are typically not as user-friendly as an intranet site.

In order to reinforce that the firm values the KM initiatives of the practice group, and to align the incentives with that objective, billable hours credit (up to a reasonable cap) should be given for that work, if at all possible.

As a further technique to keep the group's practitioners focused on making progress on the KM initiative, the firm's leaders should demonstrate their support, such as by attending some of the practice group's meetings where progress on the KM initiative is being presented. Knowing the firm's managing partner will attend the meeting should further motivate lawyers to have something to present and should improve attendance by the rest of the group.

Conclusion

Implementation is important. That's where many projects fail. Start small – with a single practice group. Leadership of that group must be seen to be actively involved. Prioritize projects according to high value and low difficulty. Gain commitment from the practice group members and employ accountability techniques, such as those described above.

It is highly desirable to create success metrics for each project. The base level should be established before starting. Devising a way to measure the relevant factors and taking measurements could take some time and may delay the start of the project, but is the only way to be able to measure comprehensively the benefits of the project. When the project is complete, measure the factors again. While the measurement process itself may involve judgments and estimates, it can nevertheless be valuable in assisting the group in deciding what works and what does not as it decides how to allocate scarce practitioner resources to KM projects.

Finally, apply successes to other practice groups.

References

1. See, e.g. Boyd, C., 'Case Study: Using Document Assembly Tools to Improve Services to Start-Ups,' Legal Tech Newsletter (Law Journal Newsletters), October 2010, available at: www.wsgr.com/publications/PDFSearch/boyd1010.pdf.
2. Oz Benamram and Sally Gonzalez, "Forming a KM Strategy for Your Firm," *Knowledge Management White Paper* (International Legal Technology Association June 2011), available at http://www.iltanet.org/MainMenuCategory/Publications/WhitePapersandSurveys/Knowledge-Management_1.html.

Chapter 2:

The "every dollar is a good dollar" fallacy – The difference between good and bad revenue

By Keith Maziarek, senior director of client value at Perkins Coie

The concept of performance measurement in the business context can take many forms across different industries. It is these measurements which provide the basis on which analysis is performed, and on which strategy and operations plans are built. Despite the varying measures of performance across industry sectors, typically an optimal and generally accepted model has been established which accurately measures performance based on the economic forces at play. Understandably this is often the result of a process of evolution over time, but mature markets have most often evolved mature methodologies by which to evaluate the relative strength of their players.

In the legal services sector, historically two metrics have dominated the conversation surrounding financial performance: realization at the matter, client, and timekeeper level, and profits per partner (PPP) at the firm level. For the purposes of our conversation here we will first focus on realization as this has been the driver of compensation and financial growth decisions at law firms for decades.

Realization is a purely revenue-based metric. Generally speaking, realization is expressed as a percentage figure, calculated as the proportion between two measures of revenue generation. There are two primary "flavors" of realization that are most commonly tracked:

1. **Billing realization** is the percentage of fees billed as a function of worked fees. This means that the fees billed will equal the fees at standard rates, less the fees worked after any hourly rate discounts are applied, less the fees associated with any write-offs of time.
2. **Collection realization** is the percentage of fees collected as a function of fees billed. This means that fees collected will be just that – revenue that has been received by the firm – compared to the fees that were billed.

There are any number of variations on how some of the data points used in these calculations can be derived, but what is constant is that these calculations only express revenues as a function of revenues. A few glaring weakness of using realization as a primary performance metric quickly come into focus, namely:

1. Most significantly, it ignores the crucial data point of cost. No matter where you set your rates or what percentage of that price you are able to collect, if you don't know your breakeven price, the percentage of your billing rate that you collect is somewhat arbitrary.
2. It is based on the relatively inconsistent reference point of billing rates, which often don't take into account market value of different services. Some services are more commoditized or more specialized than others, and as a result, command different prices as they represent different values to clients. Depending on the methodology used to set rates, if a somewhat uniform approach is used across all practices, highly commoditized services will always appear to have weak financial performance because they will have to be significantly discounted from their standard rates.

The comparative anecdote I like to use to illustrate the imprecise nature of evaluating financial performance purely as a function of revenue is a hypothetical conversation between two friends, one of which happily reports that they've sold their home. This brings up the inevitable question, "Did you get a good price for it?" If the answer to that question is, "Yes, I got 90 percent of my asking price," nothing meaningful is conveyed, because it doesn't indicate whether or not:

1. They made any money (a.k.a. captured any profit) from the sale, because you don't know what they paid for it in the first place. The price they agreed on could be lower than what they paid or owe on the loan, in which case, is 90 percent of the asking price good? It's impossible to say.
2. Their asking price was, high, low, or consistent with the market. Collecting 90 percent of a price that is 150 percent of the comparable market price would seem to be a solid gain, but 90 percent of a price that is set 25 percent below market comparable prices is nothing to brag about.

The lack of either of these reference points somewhat distorts the measure of financial performance. Realization can be a relevant data point, which is discussed later in this chapter, but on its own, it's an insufficient measure of profitability.

To be fair, the period over which realization became the focus of analysis was one of great economic prosperity in the legal services sector. Traditional law firms controlled nearly complete market share; corporate profits were high, so scrutiny over legal spend and discounts demanded were low; and large corporate clients lacked systematic purchasing frameworks aimed at achieving savings from economies of scale, and didn't engage in sophisticated, competitive bidding activities among qualified pools of service providers. Buyer power was moderate and infrequently leveraged – the legal department was run by lawyers, many of whom had come from private practice and were comfortable with the billable hour system as they had learned it. As we all know, however, times have changed.

Not all revenue is created equal

The point of this exploration of the dynamics of realization is to demonstrate that a revenue-driven metric can, and typically does, distort the evaluation of financial performance. In a revenue-only driven world, every dollar (or pound, or euro, etc.) is a good one. Financial decisions, then, can be clouded as unprofitable work is viewed as being worthwhile because it is, after all, revenue. It's a very bird-in-the-hand perspective that tends to ignore opportunity cost, as the assumption is that the first offer received is the only one available, but that is almost never the case.

To illustrate how sub-optimal financial decisions can be made when revenue is coveted and margin is ignored, consider the following case study:

CASE STUDY

A partner meets with a long-time client, and in the course of the discussion, learns that the client's financial position has weakened, and as a result, all service providers are required to freeze their rates and prices for the next two years. In this particular instance, the prices were frozen two years ago for the same reason, so the discounts afforded to this client have gotten uncharacteristically high in comparison to other similarly positioned clients. Historically this client has generated approximately $3 million in annual fees for the firm, making a compelling case to continue doing the work, because the alternative is to lose that $3 million.

The work performed for this client was spread across three practices, and the staffing mix indicated that a little over half of the work had historically been performed by senior partners. Annual rate increases for senior partners tend to be lower than those of more junior partners and associates, so while realization on the partner time – which was a majority of the worked time – had eroded over the last 4 years, it was still hovering around 78 percent. Not a traditionally healthy number, but not a crisis situation, either.

The profitability analysis of the client revealed far more troubling results, however. Given the high cost basis of senior partners and their resulting low margins, the over 25 percent effective historical discounts were producing an overall loss at the client level, with a -4 percent margin. These losses would only be amplified over the subsequent two years if rates were frozen, as the client demanded. The projected realization would dip to approximately the low 70 percent range, and margins would fall to approximately -10 percent.

The partner made the case that the alternative to not honoring the client's request was to fire the client, and that would mean losing $3 million in revenues, a preposterous proposition in his opinion. After all, while not a top performer, many clients had realization in the 70 percent range.

An aggressive case was made to stay the course and continue to commit considerable resources to this client. The net effect of the economics given the current and projected financial loss, however, mean that doing work for this client is effectively taking money out of partners' pockets as it is diminishing the bonus pool.

This summarized case study is one that plays out every day in law firms. What gets measured gets done, and the overwhelming reliance on revenue as the primary evaluation metric leads to sub-optimal business decisions.

A common argument used to justify poor financial performance is demonstrated here – if the firm doesn't do the work, how will that $3 million be generated? What will keep those lawyers busy? Because if they aren't busy, the return on their time is even lower. There is a case to be made on that basis, but it ignores the reality that there are many viable options in such situations – changing the labor mix, negotiating non-hourly pricing models with cost-efficient staffing and processes, and the obvious option of re-deploying those resources on work for other clients – new or existing – which yield a better financial return. While sometimes easier said than done, this is an important consideration that should realistically be implemented on a more consistent basis.

The case study also highlights another important element, which is leverage. Profitability varies for individual timekeepers by seniority, location, practice, and other criteria, but realization is often relatively constant, depending on the discounting agreement in place. Therefore, staffing mix can actually destroy margin while realization, and by association, revenues, would appear to justify retaining the client. This is due to the fact that a satisfactory realization figure, which is based on percentage discounts and the client's payment record, will often fuel the decision to retain a client that is, in fact, unprofitable.

One last point to cover in the case against revenue's reign that is also alluded to by the brief case study is the idea of volume. Often the argument will be made that the higher the volume of work, the more able the firm is to sustain higher discounts. Economically speaking, this is only possible up to a certain point, because there is always a breakeven point under which margins are negative. There is also the position that as timekeepers surpass their targeted billable hour requirement for the year, their costs on an hourly basis decrease. This is also an economic truth, but only up to a point, because there is a limit to how many hours a human being can work, and further, there are diminishing returns as lawyers experience burn out and work less efficiently and less accurately due to fatigue and stress. So while theoretically the volume argument can hold some validity in rationalizing high discounts in exchange for the revenue, there are limits to the value proposition.

Incentivizing the wrong behaviors

Another concerning distortion caused by exclusively focusing on any and all revenue is the misalignment of incentives it creates between firms and clients. Incentives drive behavior. When legal work is being billed on an hourly basis and revenue is what is rewarded, intuitively the timekeepers performing the work have a clear incentive to bill as much time as possible.

This incentive structure, not surprisingly, drives very predictable behaviors that are directly opposed to the best interest of the client. It incentivizes lawyers to perform work that is not necessarily vital to achieving the client's goals or objectives, to overstaff some elements of a project such that multiple people participate when fewer can ably handle the tasks, and disincentivizes efficiency in the execution of the work.

Of course the issue of ethics plays a role here, but a revenue-driven evaluation system naturally creates these motivations that can negatively impact the client.

It is easy to see, however, that the direct effect to the client is negative, which then leads to negative strategic effects for the firm. As legal bills increase, or continue to be inflated as a result of the above behaviors, clients naturally take notice and begin to audit the work more closely. The added burden of the client's constant scrutiny over invoices lowers the satisfaction with the work, and ultimately, work begins moving away from the firm. This is something of a system of checks and balances, but if balance is not maintained, the firm can lose the work altogether. Even if the work is retained, the client's diminished satisfaction and skepticism of the firm's motives does not breed a productive partnership between the client and firm.

Misalignment with customer incentives based on revenue-based goals is not exclusive to the legal services sector. Banking and financial services have demonstrated a propensity to fall into the same behaviors as well. The sub-prime mortgage crisis, and more recently, the Wells Fargo ghost accounts scandal clearly illustrate that incentivizing behaviors that contradict customer well-being can be incredibly destructive.

The cost formula

The principle of profitability has been referenced many times here, so it is likely productive to briefly address the side of margin that is traditionally a bit more opaque in the services sector – costs. In a law firm, the largest drivers of costs are salaries, benefits and real estate, generally speaking. All of these operating costs, in addition to the many other overhead costs, need to be lower than the revenues the firm collects for a law firm to maintain viability – hopefully this is not a surprise.

Many firms have developed methodologies whereby costs are allocated to each individual timekeeper in the firm based on their salary and benefits (direct costs), as well as their overhead costs such as allocations for their office, phone and data service, and the cost of back-office services like accounting, HR, and marketing (indirect costs). These costs are all allocated to each individual timekeeper to yield a total annual cost figure for supporting each timekeeper at the firm. The goal, then, is to sell their services for a sum greater than these costs.

Much profitability analysis is done at the matter or client level, so these costs must be allocated to each project. The most widespread approach for allocating costs on this basis, and thereby enabling profitability analyses, is to divide each timekeeper's annual carrying costs by some metric of their hourly annual billing targets to result in an hourly cost figure:

(Direct Costs + Indirect Costs)/Annual Hours Projected

=

Cost Rate/Hour

This provides an hourly cost rate that can be used in profitability projections against billing rates at the individual level based on their unique economic profile. Sometimes the hours are based on standardized targets by title and seniority, sometimes on historical performance, and sometimes on their pace at any given time of year that the calculations are being performed. Every firm can make a case for the methodology that is used, but profitability analysis is usually performed based on one of these costing models.

Revenue and PPP

To briefly comment on PPP in the context of this conversation, its relationship with revenue and realization is a curious one. Internally at law firms, realization has been the primary decision metric used for evaluating financial performance and the strength of portfolios of work. Partners and firm leadership will make strategic decisions based on the relative attractiveness of realization. Juxtapose this with the primary market-facing metric that is broadcast to the public – PPP – and an unusual paradox is revealed. The fact is that in many firms, there is little understanding of the relationship between revenues, realization, matter/client profitability, and PPP. This makes the incentives and behaviors proposition an interesting one, as the behaviors that are incentivized by revenue maximization, as detailed above, often contradict profitability maximization.

PPP is calculated using the classical "Revenue - Cost = Profit" formula, with the one added step of then dividing that profit calculation by the number of partners at the firm. In fact, when laterals are approached to change firms, the PPP calculation is the most fascinating data point to a prospective lateral partner. It is a signal to potential laterals on the level of compensation they can expect. Simultaneously, it is a signal from the firm to the market that can help recruit talent to the firm.

The irony is that the same partner that is considering a move to a new firm, while heavily weighting the PPP level of the new firm, usually doesn't know how the work they perform at their current firm contributes to its PPP, or even how the profit of their portfolio compares with the PPP of the prospective new firm. We won't pursue this dichotomy further here, but it is an interesting phenomenon.

Based on how PPP influences financial health of firms, if profitability is not a focus of how work is priced and how projects are staffed, PPP will fall, and as PPP goes, so goes the level of talent the firm can attract and retain. By focusing only on revenue virtually regardless of the price or margin, a firm can gradually suffocate itself. While the direct effect of the revenue-based incentives is that more cash is brought in to help "keep the lights on", the strategic effect is that the long term sustainability of the firm's service quality can be jeopardized.

A word in support of realization

Considerable time has been devoted in this chapter to discrediting realization as a performance metric, but in the interest of objectivity and fairness, realization does have some very useful applications. The main weakness relates to its focus on revenues and the loose correlation between revenues and profitability in today's price sensitive market. However, beyond the purely profit-oriented shortcomings, there are some valuable insights that can be gleaned from measuring realization.

Primary among the benefits is realization's ability to signal the extent and magnitude of revenue and profit erosion. Knowing how much elasticity is being exerted on revenues at the billing stage can help indicate where there may be a value or quality gap in a practice's offerings, where there may be inefficiencies at play, or where there may be mismanagement of the business at the practice or office level. As realization slips, an indication of the potential presence of these or other business challenges emerges, providing a basis for further diligence into the causes of the issues.

Realization as a function of collections is also a valuable indicator of revenue (and profit) erosion because it will reveal sources of cash flow interference. Such interferences are most commonly the result of clients simply not paying all of their bills. This provides evidence of a few potential causes, which could include something as simple as the client's Accounts Payable team not being particularly timely in their payment cycles, to something more systematic, such as the e-billing system not being properly configured, and of course to something more deliberate, such as the client being unsatisfied with the services.

Clients will also often use the payment cycle as a means for extracting further discounts from the firm. This happens in many cases as clients know that they have leverage over a cash accounting-based business, because once the work is completed and billed, the firm is at the client's mercy in collecting the fees. If they are short-paying their bills, the client can often bargain their way into greater savings by playing on a firm's need to collect cash to realize revenue targets. Collection realization can help identify when these issues are materializing, and help the firm to position itself to minimize the impact.

Parting thoughts

The broader business world long ago adopted profitability as a core metric of performance, because at the end of the day, every venture is in business to bring in more money than it spends. In the absence of the spend piece of that formula, financial performance and sustainability as a going concern are somewhat distorted.

Law firms' reliance on billable hours as a mechanism for not only revenue maximization, but also as a proxy for financial performance, creates a scenario where business decisions are based on only a portion of the financial picture. Revenue is certainly important, but incentivizing the billing of time as a driver of revenue reinforces some behaviors that are in direct opposition to client interests, and can be in opposition to firm interests as well if profitability is in question. The way to better align the model is to measure billable hours as a function of costs rather than revenue. This will shift the incentive to cost minimization rather than revenue maximization, and that is a much more precise practice in terms of preserving and maximizing profitability.

One of the main challenges, of course, is that familiarity with the concept of profit margin and how it is created is still relatively low among lawyers generally speaking. Once it has been explained and demonstrated, partners quickly become either fascinated or dismissive of it, depending on the picture it paints of their financial standing. As firms continue to embrace profitability as a performance metric alongside the traditional revenue-based metrics, the industry will inevitably evolve to a more mature model of targeting profitability rather than only revenue, which will help to align incentives. In the midst of that process, the best course of action is to advocate the use of profitability and to educate lawyers as often as possible, which will ultimately lower the barriers to adoption across the organization.

Chapter 3:
Pricing, profitability, and compensation

By Toby Brown, chief practice management officer at Perkins Coie

As the pricing role has been pulled into the sphere of law firm profitability, many times that pull continues on over into the compensation arena. As noted in *Law Firm Pricing: Strategies, Roles, and Responsibilities,*[1] pricing is a role that takes center stage for profitability, such that the pricing function many times becomes the voice of profitability in a firm. And once profitability is understood within a partnership's ranks, questions quickly rise about its potential role in compensation.

Discussed at length generally is the broader challenge of law firm profitability. The challenge arises since law firm partners (in the general use of the term) are both owners and workers. Any profit methodology needs to tackle the issue of how you treat partner compensation in relation to profit. Is it treated as all profit, or entirely as a labor cost? Or is it split between the two in some fashion? Whichever approach a firm takes, this first step highlights the relationship between profit and compensation, which in turn makes it clear how pricing will be drawn into the compensation dialog as it evolves.

The dialog about profit and compensation is definitely evolving and – as importantly – it will be ongoing. The underlying goal of most compensation efforts, especially outside of the legal market, is driving value and profitability.

Compensation should motivate profit enhancing behaviors and should always adapt to changing market conditions. Therefore, a prerequisite for firms is sending a clear and consistent profitability message to its partnership. Without a clear understanding of profitability, a firm cannot expect any compensation system to properly motivate profitable partner behaviors.

This law firm profit message centers on a shift from the old to the new. The old profit discussion was about hours and revenue, since that was effective at increasing profits. However, market conditions have changed, as in there is no longer increasing demand and low price sensitivity. Under flat demand and growing price sensitivity, the new discussion needs to be a broader conversation about revenue and profit. Prior to 2008, hours and revenue were enough to drive profits. But since then rate increases are down, realization against those rates has dropped from 94 percent to 84 percent, and the utilization of law firm lawyers has also dropped (increasing the cost per hour of lawyers to the firm). "Hours and revenue" is no longer effective in driving profit.

When developing a "revenue and profit" compensation system, one should keep in mind the "Law of Unintended Consequences". Compensation motivates behavior, which means there is always the problem of unintentionally motivating counterproductive behavior. Whenever a system is created, you immediately create incentives for people to game the system to their individual benefit.

Although a scary prospect when changing compensation systems, firms should realize this "gaming" is already happening under current systems. It is just that the firms are accustomed to the current gaming efforts and have in place checks and balances for tempering those efforts. New compensation systems will need to evolve to develop another set of checks and balances to keep "gaming" efforts under control.

The legal twist

In many respects, next generation compensation systems will need a component that functions along the lines of traditional sales compensation systems. This aspect will need to carefully balance protecting current revenue and profit, alongside encouraging new revenue. For those who have been involved in designing sales compensation systems, this is no easy task on its own. But here's the twist: law firms have an added a degree of difficulty, due to their owner/worker conundrum. Sales people are rarely also frontline workers. They do not build the widgets they sell. In contrast, law firm partners need to be rewarded as both workers and sales people. Both of these efforts have value for firms, but they have a different kind of value. Compensation systems will have to balance how each behavior is rewarded.

Caution

Lawyers, being Type-A personalities, tend to see things in black and white. Profit lends itself to such viewpoints. Under this thinking, profit is seen as an absolute. Practices and clients are either good or bad. As an example, a partner might see all profit below average as bad (or even failing). But profit is a mental construct and can be viewed in many different ways. For instance, costs can be calculated on either a budgeted level or an actual level. Which approach is used depends on the circumstances and goals. So, firms also need to take into account how they communicate profit in relation to compensation. Instead of being a black and white issue, profit should be communicated as having a healthy range and that the goal is increasing profits across that range. In other words, instead of using profit as a stick when it comes to compensation, it is better used as a carrot.

Of course firms should fully expect some bumps in the road as they begin to transition to different compensation systems. Effective change management will be a necessity, since changes in compensation impact the wallets of those involved. When wallets are involved, firms should expect strong reactions and proactively move to address those. Firms should also be ready to make thoughtful adjustments to compensation systems. I say "thoughtful" and not reactionary. Be prepared to adapt to core concerns, but be very careful about reacting to individual partner complaints.

One more challenge: some practices still function just fine in the old world (e.g. tax and bankruptcy) so new systems will also need to account for that.

A modest (and high-level) compensation proposal

What follows is a possible approach to developing a next-generation compensation system for a law firm. This approach breaks down compensation into a base plus three different reward or bonus buckets, allowing a firm to reward all types of profit enhancing behavior from partners. The challenge for this system, and any system like it, will be in striking the right balance between the three reward options. As previously noted, the balance will need to protect current revenue along with encouraging new revenue. Plus, it will need to properly reward key partners in order to retain them within the firm.

Baseline worker reward

First, law firm partners need to continue to function as workers. Clients hire them because of their expertise. So any compensation system will have to first account for that worker aspect. The proposed model sets a base level of billable effort (i.e. work), that all partners should reach. The exceptions (there are always exceptions) are partners with leadership and administrative responsibilities.

Further refining this concept, we might divide the base level of compensation into two or three levels, where partners are rewarded as workers. This reflects the value of partners as workers and should likely reflect their experience levels. For argument's sake, let's set this threshold at 1,000 hours. For their 1,000 hours, a firm would set base compensation for three levels (e.g. junior, mid-level, and senior partners). So, if all the partner does is bill (and collect) on the 1,000 hours, they will be paid the base amount relative to their assigned level. This base level might be treated as a "labor cost" in a firm's profitability model.

Of course, firms will set expectations that the base is not enough. Any partner functioning only at this level will likely be let go in short order since they would be only be a worker performing at a substandard level of effort.

Above the base

Our theoretical firm has three options for a partner to increase their income (and keep their jobs).

Reward option 1: Be a better worker

In this option, the partner would increase their billed and collected hours well above the 1,000 hour mark. Our future firm might set a per hour "bonus" for each partner level. Partners who fit solely into this category for compensation might be high-level subject experts, such as first-chair trial lawyers, high-value niche regulatory experts, or others with higher effective billing rates.

There will be long-term challenges with partners who only function in this role, as they are truly serving in just a worker role. They may be highly specialized or high-demand workers, but they are not actively expanding the business. Consider a star player on a NFL team. They will be paid very handsomely, but they do not make decisions about the business.

Reward option 2: Maintain an existing, valuable client relationship

Many partners at firms inherit institutional clients of the firm. Keeping these clients happy has tremendous value. Although, in a new model, keeping this client work profitable will be equally if not more important. A client that brings in \$2m in fees might sound appealing, but if it cost the firm \$3m to serve that client, there is an obvious problem. So, the compensation rewards for this option will be tied to maintaining revenue levels and improving the profitability of the revenue.

Here the compensation reward can be tied to revenue and profit levels for the existing client. A partner pursuing this compensation option will want a happy client and well-managed work. They will be concerned about practice management resources such as project management and practice innovation, and will be pushing for greater efficiencies and new value propositions in service offerings.

Reward option 3: Bring in new work

New work will come from both existing and new clients. From existing clients, this might be cross-selling new types of work or significantly expanding work in a given practice. In both circumstances, the revenue will need to be profitable or have the potential for profit. New work may initially be profit-challenged, but ultimately must fall within a firm's acceptable level of profit. Of course, adding new, profitable revenue to a firm will have the highest value and will be reflected in the compensation systems as such.

Partners pursuing this option for compensation will demand business development resources and differentiated service offerings. They will want to see efficiency enhancing efforts implemented to keep the services cost competitive, although they may not be the ones personally driving those innovations.

Combinations

Depending on the type of practice, a partner might enhance their compensation through a combination of the three options. For instance, they may choose to bill a lot and bring in new work. In any event, partners who work hard across any of the options can be properly rewarded. But those that expand the business and enhance profit will be rewarded at the highest levels.

Note that for those partners still living in the old world (e.g. tax lawyers), this new model will still be able to properly reward their efforts. Those in the old world can still be getting rate increases and work by being high-level subject matter experts. They would see rewards from all three options and thus be properly compensated.

This reward schema is different from many current law firm compensation systems, as they tend to place first emphasis on a partner's "worker" behavior at the highest value. Hard work is primarily perceived as having many billable hours. As billable hours is only one driver of law firm profit, the new models, like the one proposed here, will need to move away from that narrow thinking. Hard work comes in many other ways than just billing time. This new approach recognizes and rewards all of those efforts.

A leap of faith?

Regardless of the changes firms make to their compensation systems, they will need to find some way to balance out how they reward various profit enhancing behaviors by their partners. They may choose to place greater emphasis on one option or another, but to have an effective compensation system they will want to include all three. Leaving one out and assuming or hoping their partners will still engage in that type of behavior is ill advised. Current compensation systems reward "worker" behavior at a high level and, as a consequence, partners will focus on that effort to the exclusion of most of the others.

As a former KM professional, from personal experience I can tell you that partners (and lawyers in general) will not engage in efforts that do not impact their compensation. One example is CRM. Law firms installed expensive enterprise software systems expecting lawyers to take the time to utilize them, adding valuable client data and leveraging that to bring in more work. Lawyers, for the most part, did not participate. The moral of this story is that firms should not expect changes in behavior from lawyers unless they create a clear economic incentive for that change.

Where does that leave us? First, the traditional law firm compensation systems reward behavior that is outdated. They focus on rewards for hours and revenue. They tend to reward partners who bill a lot of hours, along with partners who bring in revenue, regardless of how profitable that revenue is. In today's market, those rewards are not sufficient to drive profitable partner behavior. Innovative firms will start altering their compensation systems to reward partner behavior that drives a profitable practice in this changing, competitive market.

References

1. Brown, T. and Cordo, V., *Law Firm Pricing: Strategies, Roles, and Responsibilities*, ARK Group, November 2013.

Chapter 4: Incentivizing the new normal

By Timothy B. Corcoran, principal of Corcoran Consulting Group, LLC

Law firms are beginning to adapt to the new world order. We're allowed to acknowledge that while the practice of law is a profession, the law practice is a business. As a business, it's subject to the same laws of finance and economics as other businesses. Law has delayed the intrusion of these practical considerations for quite some time, but even an apple falling from a very great height is still subject to the law of gravity and it will, inevitably, come to earth. Many lament the evolving business of law, but the more adventurous are beginning to recognize the wealth of information available on adapting to a changing business climate. All we have to do is translate these time-tested lessons for the unique characteristics of a law practice.

Profit is important

The first challenge is acknowledging that one primary purpose of a thriving business is to generate a profit. It's not the sole purpose, surely, but it must co-exist with other ideals and societal objectives. Generating a profit is what, bluntly, allows the firm to continue. A law firm losing money will struggle, and lawyers who should otherwise be engaged in advising clients on important matters will instead be distracted by capital calls, job searches, cost cutting, and stress. Profit allows us to invest in training, client service, pleasant surroundings for the lawyers and staff, and offer services at market prices. Profit also allows lawyers to donate pro bono time, make contributions to worthy causes, and be active in community affairs. Not only do we need to generate profit, we need to track our progress in achieving it, and we need to hold everyone accountable for their contribution. Again, it's not the sole objective of the business, but without it, we have no business.

The prevailing economic model for law firms, often referred to as the "waterfall" method, relies on several key factors to translate effort into profit. These factors are collectively known by the acronym R.U.L.E.S: realization, utilization, leverage, expenses, and speed of collections. We measure these factors as signs of fiscal health. Healthy utilization means our lawyers are working, not idle. High realization means the lawyers are billing what they work and client are paying what's been billed. Good leverage means partners delegate the work to lawyers in lower tiers, thereby generating greater profits and freeing up senior partner time for business origination. All good business keep a close eye on overhead and expenses. And as cash businesses, what a law firm collects and how quickly it collects are critical.

These factors are not the only, and certainly not the optimal, factors to measure fiscal health. But as metrics for the prevailing way law firms conduct business, they're effective. Why, then, do so many law firms de-emphasize these factors when establishing expectations for partner behavior and awarding compensation? Instead, law firms tend to track and reward a proxy that are too many steps removed from fiscal health, client satisfaction, or quality: billable hours. The first challenge facing law firms is to embrace new metrics. We must incorporate the above factors, and more, if we wish to increase the focus on the necessary outcome of law firm profitability. And we must incorporate these metrics not only in our management dashboards, but we must embed them into the partner compensation plans.

Law firm compensation plans are by and large unsophisticated, hard to administer, overly subjective, opaque, and focused on rewarding the wrong behaviors. As someone wise once said, "If your compensation plan is in conflict with your strategy, your compensation plan *is* your strategy." To generate maximum financial performance in a law firm, and achieve the highest level of client satisfaction, we need to re-align the incentives. A good plan should further the firm's strategy, be easy to administer, and both drive and reward the desired behaviors. Many miss the mark on one or more of these dimensions.

Align compensation with strategy

A simple test can reveal a common disconnect. Model the impact of all partners maximizing their personal compensation, and compare the results with the firm's strategic plan. If the potential outcome confounds rather than furthers the firm strategy, it's time to revisit the incentives. All too often the firm strategy establishes one set of goals, but the compensation plan rewards other, often entirely opposing, activities.

Example 1

Objective: Establish a market leading position by acquiring numerous new clients in certain high-growth vertical markets.

Incentive: Reward billed hours and cash receipts.

Result: By ignoring or minimizing the pursuit of new clients, for which the billed hours and cash flow may lag the business development activities, the firm clearly emphasizes that working existing client files is more critical than winning new work.

Example 2

Objective: Establish long-term many-to-many client relationships by fostering cross-selling.

Incentive: Award origination credit solely to primary relationship partner.

Result: Partners receive no credit for client expansion, so there is no incentive to contribute time and expertise to another partner's business development efforts.

There are numerous examples of misaligned incentives that work only when partners make a choice to act against their own economic self-interest. To be clear, this isn't purely a reflection on partners acting selfishly. It's easy to assume partners will always act in a "firm first" manner, but why assume? A poorly-designed compensation plan is an indictment of poor management. It's often easier to avoid making controversial adjustments to compensation and instead hope that a sufficient number of partners operate in the best interests of the firm even though firm management neglects to reward such behavior. An effective compensation plan is one that allows a timekeeper to maintain a laser focus on defined activities and incentives, so that by maximizing these incentives she or he can't help but further the firm strategy. Any misalignment is on the shoulders of firm management, not the timekeeper.

One size doesn't fit all

It's important to note that any complex, multi-line business will face different market conditions, competitive threats, cost factors, and growth potential in its various business lines. We readily comprehend that a global business such as General Electric, which makes turbine engines for aircraft in one division and light bulbs for residential homes in another, faces different competitive threats in each market segment. The strategy for the aviation division must address growing demand for more fuel-efficient engines, create products with zero tolerance for mechanical error, and its highly-trained sales force faces constant threats from Pratt & Whitney and other major players. The consumer lighting strategy must incorporate changing regulations for green power consumption into its manufacturing process, compete with low-cost alternatives from emerging markets, and rely heavily on big box retailers as a primary sales channel. It's no surprise then that different incentives are necessary for each division, and so the executive compensation plans reflect different priorities.

Why then do law firm leaders, who manage complex, multi-line, often global businesses, believe that one plan will address all the particular nuances each of its market segments poses? The litigation practice may be at the top of the market, known for delivering excellent outcomes in either the courtroom or at the negotiating table, converting bet-the-company challenges into less threatening settlements or significant public relations triumphs, and commands stratospheric hourly rates. The IP and labor practices, however, face significant price pressure as technology automates what were once lucrative engagements, and alternative providers of legal services can deliver similar outcomes at both a lower and a more predictable price. The technology practice is investing heavily in emerging growth segments like driverless cars and unmanned drones, and while engagements are still scarce it's critical to use this time to recruit subject matter experts and build capacity for the inevitable market demand. The corporate practice faces dual challenges of increasing demand for high-level M&A work, which has led to a fierce and costly war for lateral and associate talent, while clients simultaneously demand fixed fees and budget predictability, allowing second-tier players to steal market share. In what rational world would reasonable business experts agree that a single compensation plan that rewards, say, billing 1,800 hours irrespective of profit margin, price points, or competitive threats, is the best plan to address equally and simultaneously the numerous market complexities?

This isn't to say each practice group should establish its own compensation plan. Nor does this call for wholly subjective compensation plans – the kind where smart lawyers sit in a room with drawn shades and magically award compensation based on factors that are unknown to those outside the room and therefore unassailable. Rather, this calls for a compensation plan that is consistent in its structure but flexible in its implementation. The elements we reward may be the same across practices, but the emphasis may shift based on factors unique to each practice. In one practice we may dial up origination rewards, as the pursuit of new revenue is the most critical objective. In another, we may dial back origination and dial up profit margin and realization, as maintaining price integrity for our high-demand exclusive offerings takes precedence. In another, we may actually dial up rewards for business development *activities*, not results, as this might be the best way to get partners out of the office and advancing opportunities that help us build market share in an emerging area.

The formula for success

There's an endless debate as to the relative effectiveness of subjective compensation plans vs. formulaic plans. On one hand, subjective plans provide expansive flexibility, allowing leaders to make adjustments, such as rewarding cross-selling activity for a junior partner working a matter even though all origination credit accrues to the relationship partner. Subjective plans also don't tie the hands of firm leadership when something catastrophic happens, such as a key rainmaker or an important client departs, and utilization is down while everyone works to refill the pipeline. Such plans also allow leaders to reward exceptional behavior that otherwise isn't reflected in hours or receivables.

But a plan based on a formula also has many advantages. A formula is, by default, far more transparent than a subjective plan, for it declares the factors to be considered for remuneration and, hopefully, does so in advance in order to *drive* desired behavior, not just reward it after the fact. A formula plan reduces uncertainty and doubt and feelings of inequity. If, as described above, management adjusts the emphasis of individual factors for each practice based on market conditions, or even adjusts the factors based on different points in the career lifecycle – junior partners are expected to bill hours as they begin to build a book of business, whereas senior partners are rewarded for billing fewer hours while managing and delegating a large book of business – then a formula-based plan can link rewards to both behavior and opportunity, not just results.

What matters more than matters

Many partner compensation plans have some variation of these components in common: financial performance metrics; non-financial contributions; and an element of subjectivity to provide flexibility when the financial and non-financial metrics don't paint the whole picture. In some cases, the entire plan is subjective, but the compensation committee reviews and incorporates some financial and non-financial metrics in its deliberations. The financial metrics are often a proxy, measuring some facet of a timekeeper's output but omitting other important measures, such as rewarding collected receipts without considering any discounts or write-offs prior to collections, or including realized rates as a proxy for profitability without considering the long-term impact on client retention. A very high realized rate on a matter is desirable, to be sure, but not if the work is delivered at a price point that scares away repeat business.

One measure that is often notably absent is profitability. Using proxies is a starting point, but true profitability is often missing, often purposely. A partner who discounts rates at the beginning of a matter, writes down pre-bills during the matter, and offers hefty write-offs after the matter concludes when challenged by a client, should not receive rewards commensurate with another partner who keeps busy without discounts or write-offs, even if both were to generate the same net receivables. Discounts, in whatever form they take, have a disproportionate impact on profitability, which is why few businesses allow salespeople to set and/or negotiate prices without supervision. In many law firms, however, partners negotiate terms as they see fit. It should come as no surprise that partners tend not to negotiate those areas that are tracked and rewarded.

So how should we measure and reward profitability? First, let's recognize that true underlying profitability can only be measured over time. An individual client engagement might be deemed profitable using our traditional measures, but if we look at the entire client relationship we may find that actions in one matter have a ripple effect in subsequent matters. Negotiate a significant discount for matter A? Don't be surprised when the client demands that rate for future matters of this type, as well as the same discount for unrelated matters. Fail to adhere to the budget? Don't be surprised when the client shifts the work elsewhere, even if they don't complain. When we look at long-term client relationships as the goal, and not short-term cash flow, this changes what we measure and what we reward. Firms are beginning to incorporate retention rate (repeat business) and penetration rate (cross-selling) as these are highly correlated with profitable relationships. Maximizing these factors can have a profound impact on long-term profit generation.

Opaque is not the new black

Irrespective of the structure of the compensation plan, its effectiveness is greatly influenced by a factor that has nothing to do with numbers or formulae. The single greatest tactic to achieve an effective rewards system is transparency. Many firms wait until the year has concluded to tally up the results, and then dole out compensation according to overall firm performance. While this approach ensures that the rewards don't exceed the net profits, it fails miserably at guiding appropriate behavior. No disciplined management team should ever deploy resources to pursue a goal without providing – in advance – a specific goal and specific rewards for achieving, under-achieving, or over-achieving this goal.

Some firms embrace an open system, meaning that all equity partners see what others earn, in lieu of providing performance metrics. This is typically meaningless. There are so many performance factors and marketplace conditions in play, simply seeing final compensation figures provides no insights whatsoever into any one partner's relative contribution. Even if we assume that the compensation committee equitably distributes compensation, not knowing what actions will be rewarded, and in roughly what proportion, until *after* the year has concluded, is absurd. To motivate people by creating incentives requires that, by definition, people know in advance what will be measured and what rewards are available.

Without exception, firm partners will assert that the incentive plan is murky at best, and completely inscrutable at worst, while firm management will simultaneously assert that everyone is informed, content, and clear about the desired behaviors. Those not meeting the unstated expectations are considered to be under-performing and some may even receive a stern talking to in addition to seeing an impact at compensation award time. But none of this guides the partner into changing behavior; it merely frustrates the partner. When there is uncertainty, it's the responsibility of management to fix it.

Succeeding at succession

One of the most pressing issues facing law firms today, in large part due to an aging populace, is succession planning. Many firms have a substantial portion of revenue and profits under the management of partners who are at, or well beyond, the typical retirement age. Should these client relationships cease when these relationship partners step off the stage, the result would be catastrophic and nearly immediate. So it stands to reason that law firm leaders should be identifying succession plans as a firm-wide strategic priority, with all stakeholders doing their part to ensure that relationships are expanded, new up and coming partners are introduced into key relationships, and incentives are distributed in such a way as to foster collaboration. So when we examine the succession plans in many firms, we find... nothing. Crickets. Tumbleweeds. There may be much wailing and gnashing of teeth, but little is underway other than exhortations from management to "get on with it."

In lieu of a firm-wide plan, many law firm leaders have abdicated responsibility to these aging individuals, expecting them to "do what's right" to ensure the continuity of key client relationships and the revenues and profits that ensue. For a relationship partner with a fully-funded retirement account, and who therefore has no need beyond nostalgia for the firm to remain a going concern once he steps off the stage, the incentive to begin transitioning key client relationships months if not years before retirement must be financial in nature. And yet, so many plans have no provision for equitable sharing of origination or client management credit in these circumstances. The expectation is that either the senior partner will graciously forgo some compensation and transfer credit to a younger partner, or the younger partner will forgo compensation and work alongside the senior partner to transition relationships, in the hope that the client will stay and these efforts will someday, maybe, be rewarded. Naturally, absent a catalyst such as management committee intervention, these negotiations are rarely proactive and equitable. And, not surprisingly, the most benefits accrue to the outgoing partner who has all the leverage in such a negotiation. The message this sends to the younger partners is less than compelling.

If firm management concurs that client retention is a firm-wide imperative, it should fund the effort accordingly. There's a maxim in business when it comes to sharing sales credit – it's easier to feed a crowd with a larger pie. There's no reason the compensation plan can't be adjusted to provide credit to *both* the outgoing and up-and-coming partners, as both need to be rewarded for their actions and the consequences if either party fails to play along can be dire. Whatever the calculus, paying both, or "double paying" in incentive plan parlance, provides a significantly higher return on investment than whatever business development activities will be needed to replace huge revenue streams from clients who leave when partners retire. Where does the money come from? Shave a few pennies from every dollar or euro coming in the door, and fund a pool. Or take a slice off the top before profit distribution. If it's a firm strategic imperative, then everyone needs to participate, not just the partners impacted in the transition.

The new normal

One reason that many law firms haven't fully embraced project management, process improvement, or non-hourly fees, is that it doesn't pay well to do so. Despite clients demanding more predictable budgets, lower fees for routine work, leveraging the lowest cost resource capable of effectively performing legal work, and improving satisfaction, law firms are still, by and large, resolutely focused on rewarding partners who personally bill the most hours. It has never been the highest and best use of an equity partner, e.g., an *owner*, to simply bill time at an hourly rate. That's not what owners do. Senior partners should win the work, manage the relationship, ensure profitable engagements based on long-term measures of performance, and mentor the lawyers actually doing the work. Until law firm compensation plans evolve to reward this new normal, then partner incentives will continue to operate in opposition to client satisfaction. And this won't end well. A compensation assessment or redesign can be an extraordinarily effective tool to improve financial performance, foster a client-focused and collaborative culture, reduce unnecessary distractions, and provide a roadmap for career success. Expecting smart people to somehow "figure it out" is lazy management. Build the future you want in your law firm. Start today.

Chapter 5:
Managing client intake to increase profitability

By Anthony E. Davis and Wendy Wen Yun Chang partners in the Lawyers for the Profession® practice group at Hinshaw & Culbertson LLP

In the wake of the Great Recession, the legal profession has seen a fundamental and permanent change. Today, to be successful, a law firm must operate as a business while continuing to provide quality legal services. The statistics and various reports from legal services industry commentators point to the same conclusion: the total spend by corporate buyers of legal services from traditional law firms remains flat, while those same buyers simultaneously demand law firm efficiencies. Clients want more work done at a lower total cost. Unless firms adapt, this translates to smaller profit margins – or losses. In this changed world, effective client intake management is a critical tool for firms to employ in furtherance of remaining both competitive and profitable.

Client Selection

Every lawyer and law firm goes through times where economic considerations appear to favor taking any client and matter that walks in the door, on the theory that any work is better than no work. In the short term, this approach may even *feel* better, because there is work to do, leading to a false belief that profitability merely depends on the existence of work. This is not true. Profitability depends on lawyers being paid for their work at a rate that exceeds their costs of doing the work. To attain profitability, sometimes it is better not to take on every prospective client, because not every client is a good client. The best risk and client intake management systems effectively match the *right* clients for the firm and its lawyers – and identify the likely unprofitable engagements so that they can be rejected.

Properly evaluating conflicts

The duty of loyalty is at the core of the attorney-client relationship. Failure to identify conflicts quintessentially violates that duty and can lead to costly and hard to defend claims of malpractice, breach of fiduciary duty, disgorgement of fees, disqualification, and even professional discipline.

Identifying conflicts of interest are therefore the first step of every client intake decision, and every law firm has some form of conflicts analysis system. For some firms, the process is manual, where lawyers circulate the name of prospective clients amongst all attorneys in the firm, and every lawyer is required to review the information, which necessarily takes up a significant amount of attorney time. Further, because this type of manual system relies on fallible human memory, as well as a good understanding on everyone's part of the ethics rules governing conflicts, it is prone to error.

A significant proportion of malpractice claims allege both a legal error and a conflict of interest, which could, and should, have been caught and addressed during the intake process. Lawyers eager to start work ignore believing that there will never be a problem, or that they will be able to "handle" it if one arises. At the beginning of an attorney client relationship, clients are happy and the relationship is fresh. Lawyers do not think at that stage about how that relationship may sour and about the consequences if it does. A conflict that should have been addressed up front can create liability that may be independent of any claimed error. Clients routinely argue they would not have engaged the law firm had they known of the conflict. Cases where conflicts are alleged are hard to defend. Juries find them troubling, and are unforgiving. The consequences for the firm can be quite severe – liability, disgorgement of fees, damage to the firm's reputation, and potentially even professional discipline.

Laterally hired lawyers are a special risk category for firms, with particular reference to conflicts of interest. New lawyers may not be used to a rigorous intake review process, and may try to bypass it whenever they can. Strong intake systems need to be set up to make ignoring the firm's intake protocol very difficult, if not impossible. Firms should pay careful attention to lateral compliance with firm intake processes and take steps to enforce compliance from the moment lawyers join the firm.

Many firms are moving toward using automated conflicts checking software tools, where a prospective client's name is run against a database of a firm's current and former clients, identifying which lawyer handled which matter at what particular point in time, as well as names of other parties involved in the matter. A conflicts report is then generated which is reviewed either by the attorney seeking to open a new file or, more efficiently, by professional conflicts staff who are generally supervised by the office of general counsel. The analysts are trained to identify and understand conflicts, and in many instances they do understand more about the subject than most lawyers. Under the supervision of a lawyer, non-lawyer analysts can be a cost effective way of handling the conflict review process, as the analysts can process the vast majority of the conflicts inquiries, and only escalate the complex conflicts questions to the attorney seeking to open the file, and, when needed, to the firm's general counsel. This system minimizes the time necessary for attorneys to devote to the process, freeing them up to work on billable client matters – knowing they can do so free of the risks of conflicts of interest. For these reasons, these systems are more accurate, more comprehensive and much more likely to enable firms to comply with the ethics rules.

Even when the checking is done using purpose built software, in firms where the file opening lawyer is the one required to perform the conflicts analysis from the report generated by the software, it also suffers from the drawbacks that non-billable attorney time is wasted, and the critical element of independent review based on an understanding of the conflicts rules is missing.

Evaluating prospective clients for financial suitability

Historically, financial analysis of prospective clients for financial suitability, independent of the lawyer seeking to introduce the business, has not usually been a part of intake management. Law firm general counsel have not traditionally seen this as part of their responsibilities, even though they see the effects of the acceptance of unsuitable clients at the end point. But when confronted with problems associated with collections, general counsel often do wonder why the firm accepted the client in the first instance. These end point problems can be substantial, presenting ethical, legal, and financial problems. As a predicate matter, permissive withdrawals can only be effectuated if there will be no material adverse effect on the interests of the client, and after the firm has taken steps to avoid reasonably foreseeable adverse consequences to a client before that withdrawal. This may mean, in some circumstances, being ethically required to continue to provide legal services even if the client owes the lawyer substantial fees and there is little prospect of the firm getting paid. In litigation, court permission is required to withdraw, and courts may not approve the request especially if the firm waits too long to ask, leaving the firm obligated to perform legal services competently, again with no prospect of getting paid. In these situations, large accounts receivable just get bigger. Suing a client for fees is often not a viable option and is always likely to draw a cross-complaint for legal malpractice. Clients who cannot pay a firm in the first place are unlikely to be able to satisfy a judgment for fees even if the firm obtains one.

Despite these problems, firms all too often fail to draw the connection between managing the risks of bad end point consequences and making informed decisions about client selection on the front end. When general counsel try to impose financial evaluation standards on prospective clients at the front end, they face resistance from the firm's lawyers. Whoever is assigned the task of evaluating the suitability and potential profitability of prospective engagements, firms need to assign this role in order for the profitability to be assessed – independently of the lawyer seeking to introduce the business – from the firm's perspective. Further, this assessment needs to be viewed not as a roadblock to client development, but as a pathway to improving the firm's bottom line. If management is willing to recognize the value of making better front end evaluation of client suitability as a threshold matter of policy, it can then decide to assign the task either to general counsel, or to involve the firm's financial staff in establishing parameters for client financial suitability. Some firms choose a third path, creating a separate new business intake department, with input from both general counsel and the financial staff – but where the ultimate decision whether or not to accept business is shared by the general counsel and the firm's senior leadership.

Creating effective financial intake parameters requires serious effort. Initially, firms' CFOs, billing departments, and controllers need to mine their existing client data to determine the common characteristics of clients that do not pay the firm's bills. The analysis should have as its goal to identify patterns. Are problems coming from certain identifiable groups or categories of clients? For example, does a firm have a much greater problem collecting from individual, as opposed to corporate, clients? Or from certain kinds of businesses, or types of transaction or litigation? Do certain lines of business incur significant overhead costs but routinely yield no profits, or worse yet, losses?

Once the categories of unprofitable clients and matters are identified, firms can create parameters for use during intake evaluation which identify prospective matters as requiring special review and approval. For example, in what circumstance should the firm consider setting a minimum advance deposit retainer for prospective clients, and what thresholds should apply to different categories and different types of matters? Then, if prospective clients are unwilling or unable to meet the established parameters, this should be a red flag for the client's willingness or ability to pay as the matter proceed, and, absent some compelling reason, should lead to the rejection of the work.

In the post-recession world, even though tensions can be created within firms by the adoption of these sound business protocols, good risk management suggests that it is critical for firms to identify which clients are likely to be profitable, and which are likely to create problems, and to make intake decisions based upon that analysis.

A tightening legal market results in great temptation on the part of lawyers to "dabble", in other words to take on work outside their field of expertise, resulting in legal errors that lead to claims. Dabbling is also something a good intake system can manage if it is structured so as to identify who is doing what work, and permit the evaluation of whether this lawyer is the appropriate one to be handling this kind of work before the matter is accepted.

Once firms have decided to adopt this approach to client intake evaluation, the next question is what can be done to simplify, and automate, the decision making process. Software can sort matters into the suitability parameters established by the firm. The appropriate parameters for this kind of automatic screening include the following: no outstanding accounts receivable from the client; that the work to be done is the kind that the firm has the skills to perform, and is actually going to be handled by a lawyer within the appropriate practice group; and that the revenue to be generated will exceed the cost of providing the services.

On the other end of the scale, if the prospective client has no established positive history with the firm, is seeking assistance in a practice area where the firm has a negative collection experience, or is unwilling or unable to pay a retainer that the firm's financial group has identified as the minimum that is appropriate for the matter, that matter should be rejected automatically, absent specific re-evaluation by and approval of firm management.

When an intake request doesn't get a "clean" pass or fail on financial suitability after this automatic evaluation process, the request should be escalated, and reviewed by a business intake manager (or, less efficiently but common in some firms) by a committee designated to make these decisions, but in any event not by the partner seeking to introduce the business. Ultimately, client intake management should become a systematized, objective, and uniform process in which decision-making is independent, thereby improving management of the firm's risks.

Because this type of structure often involves significant changes from prior practice, risk managers need to get buy-in from the firm's lawyers and the firm's management. Lawyers are likely to comply – and may even welcome the new arrangements – if it can be shown that the time they are required to dedicate to the intake process is simplified, and that they will no longer be faced with voluminous conflict reports that are hard to read, and even harder to understand. The more the firm can demonstrate that the new arrangements will operate quickly and efficiently, consistent with the objectives of taking on good clients and weeding out bad clients, the more likely lawyers will support the system. In turn this buy-in will allow management to take the necessary steps to ensure compliance throughout the firm, based on the common objective that better client intake management will improve profitability.

Making the intake process work efficiently and promptly

The intake system must work speedily and efficiently. But in order to succeed it must receive all of the information needed on which to base decisions. If prospective new client matters are not made and communicated on an expeditious basis, lawyers feel compelled to start work, in order to avoid client prejudice (and not to lose the business). And if it later turns out that the firm decides that the matter should not have been taken it on in the first place, the firm is left with a big write-off, and a serious ethical problem in connection with withdrawal. Beyond these problems, the time it takes for the firm to sort this all out, is non-billable and entirely unproductive.

Engagement Letters/Fee Agreements

Every attorney client relationship should begin with an engagement letter. This should clearly address all of the parameters of the attorney client relationship, and should be hard wired into the intake system as a prerequisite for opening any new client engagement.

Not only will this establish uniformity, it will also simplify the process for file opening, again reducing the time needed for compliance. In addition to any terms required by ethical rules, other terms engagement letters should address are:

- accurate client identification and contact information;
- a carefully defined scope of the representation;
- identification of how and with whom the law firm will be communicating;

- circumstances for withdrawal;
- fees, costs, retainers; and
- file retention.

In addition, if the firm wishes to have an arbitration clause to aid dispute resolution (after checking with its insurance carrier), arbitration terms should be included as well.

Because the forms will be standardized and mandatory for all clients, variances from the standard form that may be needed in individual matters can be quickly identified and sent for approval to the firm's general counsel or financial manager, as appropriate.

Firms need to use the intake system to enforce the use of the approved forms. Client and matter billing numbers should not be issued, and there should be no ability to record or enter time on any matter unless and until the firm receives a countersigned engagement letter. A less onerous alternative is to assign a file number once an engagement letter has been sent to the client, but then the firm needs to monitor the matter and close it down if a countersigned engagement letter is not received within "x" days.

The requirement of an engagement letter countersigned by the client is a critical milestone in the relationship. Without a countersigned engagement letter, a law firm may find itself in the world of quantum meruit recovery for its services. More importantly, from a purely practical perspective, a good attorney client relationship is based on trust and confidence that runs both ways. If a client will not sign an engagement letter, firms must ask themselves what else will the client not sign? And if a client is unwilling to accede to the request for a countersigned engagement letter from the very beginning, what type of cooperation can the firm expect from that client in the matter itself?

Conclusion

Effective client intake takes effort and discipline both on the part of firms and individual lawyers. But once the system is up and working, a law firm can use the client intake process to create a path to improved profitability as well as saving itself serious and costly problems later.

Chapter 6:

Profitable lateral hiring – Numbers and nuances

By David J. Parnell, founder and principal of True North Partner Management

Lateral hiring gets a bad rap. The industry is full of sensational statistics that argue, and in some cases, prove, how risky, tentative, and unstable the practice can be. If you remove the substance and follow just the tenor of the lateral zeitgeist, you wouldn't consider it as a viable strategy for your firm. But, while headlines and statistics grab eyes and make great reading, reality finds its feet on the ground, which is where lateral acquisitions actually happen. And though they *can* fail, generally speaking, lateral movement nets out to be a profitable endeavor when carried out in a thoughtful and (generally) conservative way.

With a wake of industry-relevant years behind me, I've seen firms run the gamut from (a) a deep strategic process that *comprehensively* vets, profiles, financially models, courts, processes, and integrates the lateral acquisition, to (b) a willy-nilly process that comprises quick and dirty meetings followed by offers to laterals who, post-transition, are left to sink or swim. And I am confident when I say that a firm's success rate with laterals is a direct function of its placement on the spectrum between A and B; not some twist of fate's will.

If you look at the bones of the lateral hiring process and the myriad conceptual fields that pack meat onto them – cultures, values, group dynamics, governance, compensation, social-, cognitive-, and evolutionary psychology, strategy, communication, leadership, and the list just keeps going – the entire process of lateral hiring can certainly fill multiple books. A vital organ to the process is analyzing the profitability of the acquisition. We will be discussing that here, and will start out with some assumptions, first, that will help to better frame our discussion.

Assumptions

You don't cook your books

Earnings management may be defined as "reasonable and legal

management decision making and reporting intended to achieve stable and predictable financial results."[1] Companies, and certainly law firms, do this every fiscal year. And when done within the confines of generally accepted accounting principles (GAAP), it is acceptable. That said, when earnings management leans towards "aggressive," it can produce financial reports that present an overly, and potentially dangerously, positive view of a firm's financial position.

In *The Failing Law Firm: Symptoms and Remedies* I discuss aggressive accounting techniques that, while usually symptoms of the problem rather than the problem themselves, have aided in the ultimate failure of some firms over the years. These might include maneuvers such as borrowing against receivables, the removal of provisions for *definitively* bad debts, recognizing receivables as actual realizations, rearranging depreciation/amortization policies, treating operating costs as investments, and more. These are often used as short term, temporary answers to long term, semi-permanent to permanent problems. On their face, I don't advise or condone the usage of these. And I assume that you are using healthy, GAAP-compliant accounting methods.

Accountants

I assume that you use the services of a sophisticated accounting department – whether internal or external. While we will be talking about back-of-the-napkin calculations, it will be incumbent upon your firm to make a *detailed* analysis of forecasted lateral-centric cash flow – conservative/likely/optimistic – so as to make a fully educated decision on the potential acquisition.

Groups

When looking at groups, one or both of two criteria will be met: (i) the acquired book will have at least three years of historical data proving that it has kept, and will continue to keep, those included in the acquisition busy enough to meet your firms required billable hours at an acceptable bill rate, and/or (ii) your firm will have sufficient surplus work ready and waiting to absorb those that do not fulfill the first criteria. The latter applies *inextricably* to those lateral practitioners without a book.

Firm-wide strategy

You should have a sophisticated strategy in place that will act as a governing infrastructure in which to make your lateral hiring decisions. An effective and profitable lateral strategy flows from the firm's overlying strategy; not the other way around. And a properly constructed strategy will fit the following criteria: (i) a coherent plan of action, (ii) that is comprised of sufficiently proximal steps, (iii) which builds off of current strengths, (iv) that are governed by an overlying norm or policy, (v) and lead a firm from their current (practical) position to one of measurable competitive advantage. This is juxtaposed to espoused "strategies" that are in actuality just goals, or tactics, or even just values. If your firm doesn't have a solid strategy in place, you're better suited by going back to the strategy drawing board, first, and then considering your lateral needs, second.

Lateral-hiring strategy

You should have a lateral strategy in place that will comprise profiles for (i) active searches and (ii) opportunistic acquisitions. These are two different animals. For instance, searches for laterals that can slip into a predetermined need and/or surplus work may warrant taking on a bit more risk in their profile because of the higher probability for an immediate impact. Also, measuring opportunity acquisitions without a barometer can be difficult because of trance-inducing and ever-appealing inherent, but indirect advantages: synergistic opportunities, reputational signaling, client entrees, etc. There is risk in any lateral hire, full stop. It is impossible to accurately evaluate and value a lateral without a backdrop and context in which to do so.

The process of financially modeling lateral acquisitions

With those assumptions made, at this stage of the overall evaluation process, we are looking to create a 3–5,000-foot view of the finances that surround the lateral acquisition. Assuming that the lateral passes muster at this level (and meshes well on the other gate-keeping components of your vetting process), it will be incumbent upon your CFO (or other accountants) to more deeply evaluate the lateral's portable business. Depending on the profile you are considering, this may even require parsing out and modeling financials as they pertain to individual clients within the lateral's book – e.g., an overly profitable client that comprises 75 percent of an otherwise unprofitable book can easily skew numbers and present increased if not unbearable risk. With that in mind, the structure of the process follows.

Gross margin

First, we determine the reasonable yearly gross margin on the attorney's work, and, if they have one, the remainder of their book of business:

- First, (billable hours x hourly rate – pre-bill adjustments = gross billed time) x realization rate = net collections. (To keep the accounting relative simple, we aren't including cost reimbursements into net collections as they are relatively immaterial – especially at this stage).
- Now, net collections – (fixed overhead + salary/draw + benefits/employer costs) = attorney's annual gross margin (or surplus "profit" to the firm's profit pool).
- Lastly, if there is a portable book of business: (book's total revenue - primary attorney's net collections = work surplus) x firm's profit margin = book's annual gross margin.
  - Attorney's annual gross margin + book's annual gross margin = **Total gross margin**.

Costs

Second, we determine costs/expenses as they surround the yearly *production* of the lateral (and, if it exists, the support of their book) and the lateral transaction itself.

Overhead, costs, and expenses

Taking a step back, we can see that there are ramp-up costs and expenses associated with getting your lateral up and running. Let's take an optimistic view: the lateral begins work on the first day, turns in time sheets on day 30, the firm invoices on day 45, the client processes those invoices on day 60 and pays net-30. This means 90 days will go by before the firm receives dollar one for the attorney's work. Understanding that the industry generally has a collection schedule of approximately 15 percent for the first quarter, 20 percent for the second, 25 percent for the third, and 40 percent for the fourth, the 90 days can be overly generous – and particularly if we are looking at the beginning of the year. The firm will have to carry these costs until the attorney's work stabilizes. In the event that your firm has quality analytics and a history of hiring laterals, you can certainly determine a reasonable average to work with, which will be most helpful when putting together accurate numbers for your analysis.

In the case of non-equity hires, ramp-up costs and expenses are salary, benefits, and attorney overhead. In the case of an equity partner, the ramp-up costs and expenses are draw and attorney overhead, while ramp-up expenses are attorney overhead and any benefits that a firm may allot to equity partners (in the event that your firm affords equity partners any benefits). Take note that equity partner draw isn't actually an expense, which, while this will not play a role in the year-end accounting of P&L, is still material when determining the transaction's costs. To explain further, in accounting parlance, a cost can be an expense or an asset, but an expense is a cost that has expired or was necessary in order to earn revenue. These are treated differently on a balance sheet, and can (and do) impact profits differently as a result. So, with our understanding of costs versus expenses, and assuming a (generous) 90-day ramp-up, the process looks like the following:

(Attorney salary/draw / 4 = 90 days of compensation)

+ (Average fixed overhead per attorney / 4 = quarterly overhead expense)

+ (Average yearly benefits / 4 = quarterly benefits expense)

+ (Recruiter fee)

= **X ramp-up costs/expenses**

(i.e., the acquisition will cost them X to effectuate the ramp-up, and X will be a full expense at year end.)

If we are dealing with equity partners:

X ramp-up costs - draw = **Y ramp-up expenses**

(i.e., the acquisition will cost them X to effectuate the ramp-up, and Y will be the full expense at year end.)

Another material expense is the recruiting fees associated with the acquisition. Generally, the fee is 25 percent of an equity partner's projected profit share, these can be quite impactful to the bottom line.

Salary or projected profit share x 25 percent

= **recruiting fee** (an expense)

Break Even

Here, you'll look to reconcile these numbers – gross margin, ramp-up costs, and recruiting fees – to find your breakeven point and determine if the finances, along with the other aspects of the acquisition, create an appealing risk/reward picture. As should be obvious, the more firm-specific data that you can use, the more accurate this will be. You can certainly use industry standards, but those may very well skew the results in a way that can create a time bomb. Just look at the variations between firm margins in *The American Lawyer* data as an example. These numbers vary widely, and can deeply impact this analysis if your firm is a polarity on the spectrum.

Information you should gather ahead of time

Now, with this formula in our sights, there is a battery of data that you should have on hand so as to most effectively evaluate your potential lateral candidates:

Firm-specific

Fixed overhead per attorney

Query your CFO to get an average fixed overhead cost per attorney. Bear in mind, you can get as granular as you'd like with this. For instance, you may want to get fixed overhead for partners versus associates – assuming that it differs in your firm – or you might have your accountant generate a full time equivalent (FTE) standard and a multiplier for you; e.g., $150,000 per year and 0.5 for paralegals, 1.0 for associates, and 1.3 for partners. But for your purposes at this stage, I recommend simply getting an average fixed overhead figure. We will assume $200,000 per year for our calculations, which is a figure we derive from Altman Weil's 2008 paper *Report to Legal Management.*[3]

Benefits

The Bureau of Labor Statistics has the average cost of benefits to private industry at 44 percent of wages – a huge number. And as I am sure you are aware, benefits vary widely amongst firms, ranging from bare-bones packages to full medical, dental, 401K, vacation, and everything in between. This can change, dramatically, how much your firm is paying. So, you'll need to know the yearly cost of benefits per attorney in your firm, and which levels – employees vs. owners – receive benefits. While it is unlikely that your equity partners receive any benefits, your firm may have something special set up, and if this is the case, you'll need to know that in your calculations. For our calculations below, we will be using $80,000 per year.[4]

Profit margin

What is your firm's average profit margin? And if you'd like to be more specific, you can find an average profit margin on a per-practice basis. Many firms don't like to run P&L for offices or practices, but if your firm does, it can be very helpful to gaining significant clarity in your assessment. For example, as you can imagine, using a firm-wide average in a general practice firm to evaluate the margins of an insurance defense practice will be less than precise. Often enough, however, firms will use a more simplified approach at this stage due to ease of facilitation.

Average stay of your laterals

How long, on average, do your laterals stay? And don't shoot from the hip, here. Do a *numbers*-based analysis of your laterals: who came and stayed, who came and went, and for how long? What is your firm's average success rate? And once you've found your average, consider those that are still with the firm, but have been there less than the average stay. What do their practices look like? How well are they integrated into the firm?

This can be a tricky one, as if you are really looking at the profitability potential of a lateral hire, you will need to know how long you expect them to stay. Sure, sure, you "expect" them to stay until they retire. But what is the reality? If you find that a group will be netting $3 million per year after their third year with your firm but the average attorney only stays for three years, aside from having a clear vetting/integration issue with your lateral process, you are looking at a huge risk for your firm.

The book *Lateral Partner Hiring For Success*[5] states that 32 percent of UK laterals have left their firms after seven years. Altman Weil notes a median retention rate of 90 percent at the five year mark, which varies inversely with law firm size (1,000 or more lawyers = 78 percent, while 50–99 lawyers reported 98 percent).[6] For our purposes, we will use the five year mark for analysis, but you'll need to know what your average is.

1. **Typical ramp-up time**: In your firm's experience, how long has it taken your previous laterals to be up and running in full capacity? We will be using 90 days for our calculations (and many firms do use this figure for their analysis), but what has your experience been? Movement on this number can materially change your analysis.

2. **Recruiter expenses**: What does your recruiting contract look like? Industry standard is 25 percent of projected income; not draw, but projected profit distribution. Whatever your fee is, you'll need this information.

Attorney- or group-specific

Generally speaking, at a minimum you'll need much of the information that your lateral partner questionnaire (LPQ) solicits (or should solicit) and the basics that surround their book of business. In an ideal world, you will also gather more granular information about the working environment that the attorney is used to.

The lateral candidate's financial profile

Here we are looking at bill rates, hours billed, pre-bill write-downs, current and expected compensation, collections/realizations, and the typical timing of their collections. This is all of the information we will need to create a financial profile of the candidate's current and projected production, and how much, if any profit will be added to the firm's coffers. It will also be very helpful when considering how easily the lateral and/or their clients will fit within your firm's profile. For instance, while a candidate's revenue, bill rates, and compensation may fit into your firm's model, high pre-bill write downs with lower-than-normal realization rates may indicate a group of clients that are imposing extensive fee pressures that will follow to your firm.

Aspects of a portable book

What does the book, and the team that supports it, look like? How much work is portable (conservatively speaking)? What is the typical margin? How many clients, and how well diversified is the work amongst those clients? Are the clients all of a particular caliber, sector, geography, etc.? What do the individual relationships look like? (i.e., who are the relationships with? How old/deep are those relationships? Is there a personal/social component to those relationships? etc.) How many attorneys support the book, and at what level and bill rate are those attorneys? How fungible are the various attorneys? Who, specifically, manages the clients? While there are certain aspects that are vital to a financial analysis – e.g., how many attorneys support it? How many are equity partners? What are the various bill rates? etc. – much of the other information offers a solid litmus test for eyeing up the portability, stability, durability, and compatibility of the book within your firm.

Working environment
Here we are looking for a picture of the lateral's current practicing environment. What are the typical margins at their current firm – both practice-specific and firm-wide? What policies, specifically (if any) surround financial hygiene? Do the attorneys follow those policies, tightly? What does their current compensation model look like? Does it promote collaboration or siloing? What aspects of the practice are most heavily incentivized? How much, on average, is their firm paying on a book of business? Is there synergy between groups and/or offices? Can they describe their current firm's culture? Etc. The more comprehensive your picture of their current environment, the better the scale you'll have to forecast compatibility within your firm.

Performing the analysis

Non-equity partners

Let's first consider a non-equity service partner that fits your strategy but has no book of business. This is a skill-set hire: you have surplus work for this attorney that they'll be slipping right into, and at first blush, they fit all of the criteria you've been seeking – practice, experience, caliber, etc. Based on historical workflow and current surplus, you expect this hire to bill 2,000 hours at a bill rate of $700 per hour. All things considered, ramp-up should be very quick. And while integration will be important, the process of internal networking is of less immediate importance, and there won't be the responsibility of transferring files, extra care given to client portability, etc. That said, let's outline the necessary information.

Attorney info

- Their expected bill rate and hours: $700 per hour and 2,000 hours per year.
- Your firm's average pre-bill write-downs is 5 percent.
- Your firm's average realization rate is 93 percent.
- Proposed compensation is $440K per year.
- Expected portable billings are N/A.
- Your firm's margin is 35 percent.

Determine gross margin

At a $700 per hour bill rate and 2,000 hours, the lateral would generate $1.4M in gross revenue. Let's assume that you have average pre-bill write-downs of 5 percent, and realization is typically 93 percent (assuming both from your firm's historical data).

Partner revenue:

(2,000 hours x $700 bill rate = $1.4M in gross production)

- (5 percent pre-bill write-downs = $1.33M in net billings)

x (93 percent realization rate)

= $1.24M in net collections

Partner expense:

($200K fixed overhead + $440K salary + $80K benefits)

= $720K yearly expense

Gross margin:

($1.24M net collections)

- ($720K yearly expenses)

= $520K of gross margin ("profit") for the firm on a yearly basis

This sounds great at first blush, but we still need to reconcile expenses.

Acquisition expenses

Ramp-up and transaction expenses:

($440K salary / 4 [90 days of compensation] = $110K)

+ ($200K fixed overhead / 4 [quarterly overhead expense] = $50K)

+ ($80K benefits / 4 [quarterly benefits expense] = $20K)

+ (25 percent recruiter fee X $440K = $110K)

= $290K in total 90-day ramp-up and transaction expenses

Break even?

When is our break even? Well, we need to consider that no money will be collected for (at least) the first 90 days. With this in mind, actual first year collections will be ($520K gross margin) - (net collections of $1.24M x

25 percent = $310K) = an *actual* gross margin for first year of $210K. Subtract from this the total ramp-up expense of $290K to get a first-year expense of $80K. With expected yearly gross profit margins of ~520K, this hire would break even the fifth quarter of employment, and assuming that you have a history of laterals staying at least two years, this will become profitable.

Equity partners

Now let's consider an equity partner with a $3 million business book that is leveraged to three other associates, but no one else is coming along with them.

Attorney info

- Their current bill rate is $950 and their three year average billable hours is 1,900. You expect these to stay the same in the transition.
- Their pre-bill write-downs are 8 percent, and their current realization rate is 93 percent; both are acceptable.
- Their current compensation is $900K.
- Their expected portable revenue is $3M.
- The typical margin at their current firm is 35 percent. (We will use their margin to assess at this stage.)
- The capital contribution at your firm is 35 percent. Assuming a $900K profit projection, their contribution will be $315K.

Determine gross margin

Equity partner revenue:

(1,900 hours x $950 bill rate = $1.8M in gross production)

- (8 percent pre-bill write-downs = $1.66M in net billings)

x (93 percent realization rate)

= $1.54M in net collections

Equity partner yearly cost/expense:

($900K compensation)

+ ($200K overhead)

= $1.1M per year in costs/expenses

Gross margin:

($1.54M net collections)

- ($1.1M in yearly expenses)

= $440K gross margin per year from the equity partner's work contribution

Margin on the rest of the book:

If the book is $3M, then subtract $1.54M in partner collections from $3M = $1.46M in surplus work. Multiply this by your firm's standard profit margin of 35 percent = $511K.

Total gross margin - (equity partner gross margin of $440K + remainder of book's gross margin of $511K) = $951K of yearly gross margin to the firm.

As an aside, this is a total book profit margin of 32 percent, which isn't ideal, but it certainly is within earshot of your firm's 35 percent.

Acquisition expenses

Ramp-up and transaction costs and expenses:

At a 55 percent draw rate on projected income, we have: ($900K x .55 x [.25 for 90 days' ramp-up] = $124k) + ($200K fixed overhead / 4 [quarterly overhead expense] = $50K) + ($0 for benefits, as equity partner will be paying their own) + (25 percent recruiter fee X $900K = $225K) = $399K in total 90-day ramp-up and transaction costs.

The actual expense, however, is less because the partner distributions are not a "salary," but advances against the partnership profit pool, so while the firm is fronting the $124K for the first 90 days (a "cost"), the actual 90-day ramp-up expense is ($275K) because the $124K winds up being a distribution of profits at year's end.

Break even?

Again, assuming a start date at the beginning of the fiscal year, only 75 percent of net collections will come in the first year. This means that the first year's actual gross margin will be $951K - ($3M x 25 percent = $750K) = $201K in profit to the firm in the first year. At least on the surface, this looks like a great hire. And while this acquisition also comes along with a capital infusion, that capital won't come into play, here, because it just isn't necessary. We'll talk about capital a bit more in the coming sections.

Groups

Now let's up the ante: we'll consider the acquisition of a group with a single alpha equity partner, four service equity partners (compensation is $750,000 per partner per year), four non-equity partners (compensation is $450,000 per partner per year), seven associates (compensation is three times $210,000 per associate per year, two times $280,000 per associate per year, and two times $315,000 per associate per year), and a $20 million book of business.

Attorney info: Alpha equity partner

- Current bill rate is $1,100 per hour and three year average on hours billed is 2,100.
- Pre-bill write-downs are 5 percent.
- Realization rate are 95 percent.
- Current compensation is $4M.
- Expected portable revenue is $20M.
- Typical margin at current firm is 35 percent.
- Capital contributions are 35 percent.

Note: If you are under the gun, as a very quick-and-dirty method for gross margin on a book, you can simply multiply the book by their firm's profit margin – here giving us $7M. But if you are working in the spirit of due diligence, which you should be, you'll want to at least take into consideration the profit share of the alpha partner. While the supporting nuances to the following assertion can be myriad and deep, generally, the alpha is the one with the negotiating power, and it is usually only their compensation that can *materially* impact the profitability of the book. Service partners and associates, while important, often have much less horsepower in the way of negotiating, and as such, should the acquisition unfold, you can assume that their compensation will ultimately fall in line with your firm's established RPL and per-attorney profit margin.

Determine gross margin

Alpha equity partner revenue:

Production at their current firm (and therefore expected post-transition production):

(2,100hrs x $1,100 bill rate = $2.31M in gross production)

- (5 percent pre-bill write-downs = $2.19M in net billings)

x (95 percent realization rate)

= $2.1M in net collections

Alpha equity partner yearly costs/expense:

($4M compensation) + ($200K overhead)

= $4.2M per year in costs/expenses

Alpha equity partner gross margin:

($2.1M net collections)

- ($4.2M in yearly costs/expenses)

= -$2.1M gross margin per year from alpha partner's production

Margin on the rest of the book:

If the book is $20M, then subtract $2.1M in alpha partner collections from 20M = $17.9M in surplus work. Multiply this by the standard profit margin of 35 percent (firm's average pm) = $6.27M gross margin on the book.

Total gross margin - (Alpha partner gross margin [-$2.1M + remainder of book's gross margin [$6.27M]) = $4.17M yearly profit to enterprise.

As you can see, this is around 21 percent of the book, as opposed to the quick and dirty $7M (35 percent standard margin) we applied earlier. The alpha partner's compensation has a material impact on the gross margin. This doesn't automatically make this a bad acquisition, however, so let's dig deeper to see what the entire transaction looks like.

Acquisition expenses

Ramp-up and transaction costs and expenses:

Equity partners:

At a 55 percent draw rate on projected income:

($4M + [4 X $750K] = $7M) x (.55 x .25 [for 90 days]) = $963k

+ (fixed overhead is $200K per attorney x 5 / 4 = $250K)

+ ($0 – equity partners are assumed to pay their own benefits)

= equity partner ramp-up cost of $1.21M

Non-equity partners and associates:

((4 non-equity partners x $450K = $1.8M / 4 = $450K)

+ ([3 associates x $210K = $630K] + [2 associates x $280K = $560K]

+ [2 associates x $315K = $630K]) = $2.27M x .25 = $568K))

+ (fixed overhead is $200K per attorney x 11 / 4 = $550K)

+ (benefits/employer expenses are $80K per attorney x 11 / 4 = $220K)

= attorney ramp-up expenses of $1.34M

Recruiting expense:

Associates are, generally speaking, no longer paid for in group moves. So, the partner recruiter fee is:

25 percent of ([alpha partner = $4M] + [4 service equity partners x $750K a piece] = $3M)

+ (4 non-equity partner x $450K = $1.8M) = ($8.8M x 25 percent)

= $2.2M in recruiting fees

Total ramp-up and transaction *costs and expenses* for first 90 days = $4.75M

Remember, though, that the actual expense is less because the equity partner distributions are not a "salary," but advances against the partnership profit pool. So, while the firm is fronting the full $4.75M (which includes the $963K for equity partner ramp-up draws), the actual profit-impacting expense at year end is ($4.75M total costs - $963K of profit distributions to the 5 equity partners) = $3.79M in total first year *expenses*.

Break even?

In a *full* year of production, we are looking at $4.17M in gross margin. If we remove the full $3.79M in ramp-up and recruiting *expenses*, we get $38K in gross margin to the firm at year end, which isn't too shabby considering the gravity of the acquisition in years to come. But, assuming a start date at the beginning of the fiscal year, we will only get 75 percent of collections in the first year: $15M. So, adjusted gross profit for first year is $4.17M - $5M = -$830K in first year revenue. Add to this the $3.79M of ramp-up and recruiting expenses, and you get a $4.62M loss in the first year.

Modifying the transaction

This (huge) negative balance in the first year brings us to the real meat of this chapter: modifying the acquisition – within GAAP-compliant standards and to the long-term benefit of the firm – so as to ensure that the transaction isn't negatively impactful on year-end profits.

Now, if you take a step back and look at the big picture, this massive red line shouldn't be very troublesome; particularly if we are viewing the acquisition in the context of the *corporate* world. Even at a $4.62 million loss in the first year, the potential acquisition – assuming that their post-transition cash flow quickly stabilizes and continues to produce at the agreed-upon levels – will turn profitable within another five quarters (nine quarters in total) and will be contributing less than $4 million a year to the firm thereafter. Even if they wind up leaving within four or five years, they will have been at least a financial boon – notwithstanding the intangible effects of sustaining the eventual lateral loss of the group.

But, we cannot underestimate the importance of the transaction's impact on the firm's reported profits. In *The Failing Law Firm: Symptoms and Remedies* I spend an entire chapter discussing the impact – both internally and externally – that advertised PPP have on a firm. If we are speaking plainly – i.e., removing any moral, ethical, or even just idealistic argument – while there exists myriad anecdotal, and in some cases, empirical, data to support the following statement, please accept this: PPP are terribly important figures in the legal markets. And with that in mind, there are some things that we can do to modify the accounting a bit to reduce, or even remove, the "loss" in the first and subsequent year(s).

Capital contributions

Getting back to our group, while the upfront expense of the transaction will cause a $4.62 million hit to this year's profits, let us not forget that the five equity partners will be contributing $2.45 million to the firm's capital coffers (35 percent of $7 million). As should be obvious, this is an asset on the balance sheet, but isn't income, and as such can't be used as cash flow to offset the expense. It can, however, be used to "pay down" the incurred expenses, which, in this case, will basically take away a bit more than half of the incurred expense, leaving us with a $2.17 million first year loss.

If the group continues on its pace of adding $4.17 million in gross revenue to the firm per year, assuming stabilized cash flow in the post-transition years, the firm (and the group) will have achieved a "break-even" by the third quarter of the group's second year (seven quarters in total), with the firm having paid back the expended $2.45 million capital contributions to the balance sheet by around the first quarter of the third year (again, nine quarters in total).

Does this help? Yes, in a way. It lessens the first-year impact. But does it wipe away the impact? No.

Amortization: Modified cash basis accounting

In a $1 billion law firm, this kind of first year impact may not be enough to create concern: assuming there are material improvements to the firm's strategic standing and/or brand as a result of the acquisition, they will make the hire, take the small first-year loss, and move on. But what if you are a $200 million firm? What if you are a $50 million firm? $2.17 million is quite material to your bottom line and will glaringly show up in your reported profits. This is where we look to use modified cash basis accounting to capitalize the recruiting fees and first year ramp-up expenses.

Assuming you are not an accountant, here is a bit of an explanation: Where cash basis accounting records transactions *only* when cash flows in or out, accrual basis accounting records transactions when revenue is earned (and not necessarily received) and when expenses are incurred (and not necessarily paid). Cash basis accounting, on the whole, will keep the firm on a straighter path, and helps to avoid potential issues that can arise out of overly positive earnings management. That said, modified cash basis accounting seeks to find a happy medium between the two methods, and can allow a firm to take advantage of a long-term opportunity while easing the pain of a transaction like this on their year-end reports.

In this case, the firm could capitalize the recruiting expenses – $2.2 million – to heavily reduce the impact. To amortize the fee, you should use (at least as a guide) your firm's historical data (as it surrounds the average time laterals stay) so as to determine your "useful life" of the asset. Again, referring back to the 2011 Altman Weil survey *Law Firms in Transition*, we will use five years, here. But, if your median lateral stay is less than five years, use your median number; if your median is more, use Altman's five years. Although we are reading the tea leaves a bit here, we also want to take a conservative approach, as you don't want to wind up with a couple million in deferred expenses when the lateral is on their way out the door.

So, if we amortize $2.2 million over five years, we get $440,000 per year, and our first-year total expenses are reduced to:

$4.62M - $2.2M = $2.42M + $440K = $2.86M

And if we use the capital contribution of $2.45 million to reduce the $2.86 million, we are left with $41,000 in first year recordable expenses. This is a much more palatable position.

But, what if you can't afford for this transaction to impact first year profits at all? Perhaps your firm has seen a couple of down years, and while this strategic hire is very important to the future of the firm, another year of (even just a minor) loss can mean the difference between keeping and losing important people. Does this sound like an unlikely situation? It may to some. But I have seen firms in a tenuous spot like this. And while $41,000 certainly seems immaterial, depending on the size of the firm – or, expanding the hypothetical, the size of the recordable expense when the recruiting fee has been amortized – a firm many need to go further. With that in mind, we can look to also capitalize the expense of the entire transaction: $3.79 million / 5 = $758,000 in first year expenses. And by using the acquisition's capital contributions to pay for this, the acquisition becomes much more appealing. You could, if you'd like, amortize the entire $4.62 million – all costs and expenses – but I don't think we'll need that here.

If you recall, gross revenue was still going to be reduced by 0.25 in the first year, leaving us with -$830,000, notwithstanding recruiting and ramp-up expenses. So, in this case the first-year *costs and expenses* will be:

$830K + $758K = $1.59M

But by using the equity partners' capital infusion to pay down those first-year costs and expenses – and not a penny more – *technically* the acquisition is placed into the black within the fifth quarter of their arrival (if the firm delays payback of the capital to the firm's coffers). But, assuming that workflow and cash flow is stabilized in the following years, and the firm is set to replenish the capital contribution in year two, this will bring in $1.82 million in gross margin for quarters five to eight, with a breakeven somewhere early on in the seventh quarter:

> [$4.17M in gross profits] - [$758K in amortization expense + $1.59M in paid back capital expenditure = $2.35M] = $1.82M
>
> and
>
> $3.241M in gross margin for the following three years ($4.17M - $758K = $3.41M)
>
> and
>
> $4.17M in gross margin per year thereafter (assuming consistent work-flow/cashflow, and no developments in the group's book)

Is this a good hire?

That depends. As with most everything in life, you are building a decision model based on pitting risk against reward, and while this chapter focuses on lateral finances, we'd be fools to posit that a decision can be made in a financial bubble. There are many other nuances that come into play: what is the actual stay time of lateral acquisitions at your firm, and how do the finances relate to that? What are the histories and current states of each client relationship within the book? How do the client profiles match up with those of yours? How close are the various bill rates with your firm's prevailing norms? What client entrees might occur as a result of the acquisition? How might the acquisition be used as a marketing piece? How else can the skill-set(s) be used in supporting your existing clients? Is there a cultural reinforcement that comes along with the acquisition? What will it do for morale? What will this signal to the market? And the list goes on… Answering these questions, alone, can fill a book. Acknowledging that, let's refocus on *finance-related* nuances that you can add to your decision model.

Compensation

I hear it time and again from laterals: "My move isn't a money grab." And while that is often true, don't fool yourself about compensation: it *is* important, full stop; but it is also often negotiable. The more a firm has to offer in the way of brand recognition, the quality of their talent pool, their track record of strong risk management, etc., the less it actually has to "pay" to get talent (relatively speaking). This correlation doesn't just run linearly off the charts; meaning that the top firms pay very little for the best talent. But, they do have other chips to negotiate with aside from money, and often find it much easier (and more comfortable) to fit the lateral into a smaller partnership spread (ratio of highest to lowest paid partner) than other firms.

Looking at our hypothetical group's alpha, for example: $4 million on a $20 million book decreases the profit margin considerably. If we drop the $4 million to $3 million, we will bring the book's actual working profit margin up five points to 26 percent, and shave $250,000 in recruiting fees off of your first-year expenses. Is this possible? Maybe, depending on what else your firm has to offer. Your CFO can play with different scenarios to (i) provide you with negotiating positions, and (ii) give you objective data to explain those positions to your lateral/s, which is always helpful when conveying a package.

Winnowing the group

How badly does the group need the associates? The income service partners? The equity service partners? How much surplus could your firm absorb if one, two, three, or all of the group were removed? This is a highly nuanced process – negotiating who actually comes along in the move – but is a really important one. Think of it like this: generally speaking the less people that are acquired and the more work that is captured/absorbed and processed by your existing attorneys, the more profitable the group will be to you. It will immediately reduce ramp-up and recruiting costs, and in the event that you are not currently utilizing attorneys to full capacity – thus, negatively impacting your firm's current profit margin – you will immediately generate more profit. So, with rapport, tact, and skill, you will want to understand the dynamics of the group to see if it can be winnowed.

Utilization

There are four equity partners in this group. This teases the question: how efficient is the alpha's utilization? Can some, or even much, of the work be pushed further down the leverage chain? Or, can some of the associate's work be brought up to under-billing, more senior people that can do the work and charge higher bill rates? You will want to understand the kind of work that each stratum is doing, and with the help of the alpha, attempt to map the efficiency of their utilization. This is part and parcel to winnowing the group, and if better utilization can be achieved, it may show up in a more detailed, granular analysis of the prospective book.

Recruiting fees

Post 2008, many, if not most, firms are no longer paying recruiting fees on associates in groups. I've also noticed some firm's placing fee caps on group placements, as well. Make no bones about it: a fee cap sends a signal to the market. I say this understanding full well that I, a search and placement professional, benefit from the absence of fee caps. With that said, these caps can send the same type of signal to the market that any other expense-reducing efforts will: "Why is the firm reducing expenses?" To the corporate world this concept may sound ridiculous, but in the legal market where many firms have traditionally made their brand (in part) on spending lavishly, there still exists the specter of this cultural value, and some firms continue to shun caps as a result. But if fiscal responsibility is more important to you than unbridled prestige – which is where the market has been headed for a long time – you might want to consider placing a $1.5–$2 million cap on your group hires.

Handling capital returns

A sizable amount of risk can come in the form of an early departure combined with a quick return of the lateral's capital. Imagine capitalizing the aforementioned group's recruiting fees and ramp-up costs, paying the amortization down with their capital, and then having the alpha depart with the other equity partners a year later. You'd be left with overcapacity – sure – but you'd also be on the hook for returning the $2.45 million in the same year. If you don't have a provision in your partnership agreement that extends – as much as is reasonable – the return of partner's capital, put one in. Aside from breathing room, you also add an incentive for teetering partners to stay and focus on fixing, rather than fleeing, their qualms.

Financial hygiene

You'll want to compare, in detail, your firm's financial hygiene – both proposed and actual; there is often a difference – and the policies that exist (or don't) to support it. This is so that you can compare yours with that of the group in consideration. Consider accounts receivable, for instance: if you are a $650 million firm, your work day collections are $2.5 million. A five day per year slower collection process means

$12.5 million less to the firm. In a partnership of 180 attorneys, this means $70,000 less at the end of the year. 10 days slower? $25 million less, and $140,000 less to each partner. Further, $25 million could easily mean the difference between an increase or a loss in the firm's PPP trend. Collections matter; so do client intake procedures, handling of work in progress, attitudes toward and policies about pre-bill write downs, late payments, or even just turning in timesheets. All of these, and more, can give you a good idea as to what the post-transition day-to-day will look like.

So, what does the group's financial hygiene look like? Will it be problematic if brought into your firm's fold, as is? Do they recognize that it can be optimized? If so, what and how can it be optimized? Is this something worth fixing, or is it better to be avoided?

Business plan

While the business plan relates directly to the finances of the potential acquisition in that it (should) spell out the lawyer's/group's LPQ numbers, there are also important nuances to consider. I've worked with some of the best firms in the world; especially where lateral recruitment is concerned. If there is one common thread I've found, it is that the business plan they put together during the courting process – often a collaborative function with the lateral – is, in essence, the blueprint for the post-transition integration. It not only maps out, in depth, the lateral's entire book of business and the market that they serve, it also creates the firm-wide matrix for introductions, synergy plans, drop lists of potential opportunities, transition plans – including the existing attorney teams waiting to pick up work – and more. These are not business plans; these are BUSINESS PLANS! And while vetting is important, the speed with which clients are transitioned and that the work begins to stabilize is an incredibly important piece of the profitability puzzle. A detailed and highly granular business plan – ideally with a proposed temporal infrastructure – is the blueprint for making this happen.

Start date

As you may have considered by now, a start date late in the fiscal year can have a very deep impact on the transaction. A start in the very beginning of a fiscal cycle (generously) implies receiving only 75 percent of the book's total collections for the year. What if a group transitions midway or late into the fiscal cycle? This can have a very heavy impact on the analysis, and can possibly be deep enough that capital contributions won't cover the expense, leaving the firm to dip into (i) capital reserves (affecting the balance sheet, but not profits), (ii) a line of credit (affecting the balance sheet but not profits in a material way), or (iii) actual profits.

So, when will the group be starting? And if it is not in the beginning of the fiscal cycle, how will the finances look? And, is the actual transition of the group negotiable without a material increase in the risk of potentially losing the group to a competitor?

Summary

Getting back to our group – is this a good acquisition? As I said earlier, that depends. If your firm has a poor track record of keeping laterals long-term, generally has to over-pay for books of business, is set to absorb the entire group, has poor utilization with sloppy or toothless policies that surround financial hygiene, pays high recruiting fees, immediately returns capital after departures, has notoriously shallow, sloppy, and altogether useless business plans, and the group is starting toward the end of the year, I'd say that this group is probably too risky for you. But if you have a decent track record of keeping laterals long-term, vet this group thoroughly, and can perhaps negotiate a few of the points mentioned here, I'd say that with some accounting provisions and a bit of luck, this will be a wonderful addition to your bottom line. I say that knowing full well that very few firms sit on one of these two polarities. And while you've been given some tools in this chapter, it will be up to you and your committee to use these tools and the various other gatekeeping criteria that surround them to find your potential acquisition's placement on the spectrum of risk and reward.

References

1. McKee, T., *Earnings Management: An Executive Perspective*, Page 1, Texere 2005.
2. Reeser, E., "Anatomy of Big Law Firms' Demise: How Did It All Happen?", *L.A. Daily J.*, July 2009.
3. Altman Weil, *Report to Legal Management,* November/December 2008, Volume 36, Numbers 2/3, Page 1.
4. Bureau of Labor Statistics, U.S. Department of Labor, *The Economics Daily*, "Employer costs for employee compensation", March 2015 See: http://www.bls.gov/opub/ted/2015/employer-costs-for-employee-compensation-march-2015.htm.
5. Brandon, M., *Lateral Partner Hiring for Law Firms: Hiring for Success*, London: ARK Group 2013.
6. Altman Weil, *Law Firms In Transition*, 2011.

Chapter 7: Measuring different practice groups, differently

By Michael Roster, co-chair of the Association of Corporate Counsel's Value Challenge Steering Committee

Clients have long said: "I hire the lawyer, not the firm." Through this simple phrase, the market has been telling law firms something they have largely ignored. If they would only stand back and listen to what clients are saying, the firms would also see a blueprint for improved and sustainable profitability.

Client purchasing decisions

In meetings with clients and law firms, I often put on the screen a slide showing the logos of widely different companies that are all part of Procter & Gamble (Bounty, Braun, Charmin, Gillette, Pampers, Vicks, etc.). I note that no one goes into a store and says: "I love Bounty, what else does P&G make that I can buy?" Yet law firms continue to market themselves as if their "brand" somehow means clients will buy from them lots of other legal services (litigation, labor law, securities compliance, etc.) when in fact that rarely happens. As with a customer buying a certain product from one of P&G's many brands, the client has likely selected a particular lawyer – or, more to the point, the practice group, since a client's work is typically handled by a close-knit team – rather than the firm.

Just as shoppers choose among brands of paper towels, small appliances, razor blades, and the like with a very independent evaluation of each type of product, not who makes it, clients might use the services of other practice groups at a firm based on the pricing and quality of that group, but not because the group is part of the same firm.

I then show another slide with the logos of companies that are part of Volkswagen Group. I note that while a Bentley or Bugatti might sell for $250,000 up to $2 million versus a VW Jetta that starts at around $20,000, only a small number of the high priced cars are sold each year versus over nine million Volkswagens. However, no one running Volkswagen Group would say, "let's dump the lower priced Volkswagen brand and only sell Bentleys and Bugattis", yet that's how too many law firm leaders are running their firms. They favor practice groups that charge the highest hourly rates and bill the most hours, versus groups that can generate true and sustainable profits.

If we focus on practice group profitability, we should also recognize that some practice groups might actually be more profitable if they *reduce* their hourly rates (or, more to the point, their cost of production). That is, they might focus on how to be significantly more efficient; how to shift from billable hours to fixed prices for tasks, matters, and portfolios; and how to be rewarded by pricing themselves in ways that competitors can't readily match, even as the practice group's own profitability increases significantly.

The firm as a provider of space and services

When meeting with law firms, I likewise suggest that they are not like corporations that should be run from the top down. Rather, they are much more like medical centers, universities, and similar entities that provide space and support services to widely divergent groups of professionals.

Yes, people recognize the Sutter Health, City of Hope, Harvard, Stanford, and similar brands. But, in reality, the surgery versus dermatology departments, or the history versus physics departments, will be evaluated very differently by third parties – that is, by prospective patients or students, as well as by the doctors and faculty members who might base their professional careers there.

The same is true for legal services. To continue my analogy, whereas the billings for surgery and the compensation to surgeons is usually quite high as compared to comparable numbers for dermatologists, at many medical centers surgery can be a money loser, versus dermatology that is typically in high demand and highly profitable.

For lots of reasons, medical centers and universities need to offer a wide range of services. Not all services will be rated in the top tier, and the organization's leaders will regularly watch for any departments that might be underperforming in various ways (external rankings, profit margins, ability to attract the desired talent, etc.). That said, management knows that the various services need to be priced differently, compensation needs to vary widely, and how the individual departments operate thus will be quite different one from another.

Markets and perceptions

What this means for law firms is to stop running themselves internally, and marketing themselves externally, as if one size fits all. Recent discussions with general counsels of companies, both large and small, has led to a remarkably similar observation. They all increasingly comment that 15 percent of their companies' legal spend (not individual matters, but total legal spend) is not at all price sensitive. A particular corporate transaction or a particular piece of litigation is sufficiently important that no one cares about the legal costs. And of course, most law firms want to get this work.

But firms need to be careful not to get overly focused solely on the premium work because the reality is, the remaining 85 percent of legal spend is now extraordinarily price sensitive.

For any given matter, or even a whole portfolio of matters, there are typically 10–20 highly qualified lawyers and practice groups who are competing for the work. So of course the client is going to make the selection largely based on price. That doesn't mean that the cheapest firm will get the work. There are lots of qualities a client will consider. But the practice group needs to be very competitive in price or it has no chance.

There's a related dynamic that is emerging. Law firm leaders put significant emphasis on the premium work, yet corporate clients increasingly are ranking their law firms by cost. Several companies have started ranking firms on a computerized management system with one to four dollar signs or something similar, with a rule that no one can use a three- or four-dollar sign law firm without the explicit approval of the GC.

What does this mean to a firm? Possibly if a law firm got a bet-the-company matter and did a great job, it may also now be rated internally by the client with three- or four-dollar signs. So while a firm was highly regarded and well compensated for the premium matter, it is now out of contention for almost everything else, absent a specific waiver from the GC. And no matter how hard other practice groups might try to cross-sell, they are up against comparable firms and practice groups that don't carry the stigma of being labelled a three- or four-dollar sign firm.

Some law firm leaders also forget the important benefits that come from doing non-premium work. First, that work is typically long-term and sustainable. That is, if a practice group is doing regulatory compliance, it's not likely the client is going to change providers absent significant shortcomings. Plus, it's an important revenue stream for the firm, provides predictable cash flow, helps train the junior lawyers, and helps cover the firm's overhead.

More importantly, that daily and ongoing work continues to enhance the expertise of the practice group, and thus can put the firm into contention for the bet-the-company, premium work – not just for this client, but in the market overall. As I used to tell the lawyers in my financial institutions practice group at Morrison & Foerster, "it helps to know something". Because we did so much basic bank regulatory work, we were also very much in contention for the significant enforcement matters, class actions, and the like. We and related practice groups at the firm, through the daily housekeeping work we did, often knew substantive details that the law firms that only did premium-level work would not know or even understand the implications of.

Other ways practice groups differ

From the outside, client and market perceptions are an important differentiator. As a general counsel, if I didn't already know which firms and lawyers I'd consider for a new type of matter, usually my first inquiry would be with other general counsel. Who were they using? What did they think? Where did firms fall short? Where were firms strong?

There's also the issue of how much work is available. Virtually all practice groups have up and down cycles. But over the long haul the question is, what is the likely amount of work the practice group can reasonably expect to obtain, and how should that, in turn, affect how the practice group prices and staffs itself? The bitter truth that too many lawyers and firms keep ignoring is that, with a surplus of very high quality lawyers, lawyer incomes may need to come down unless the relevant practice group can somehow improve profitability while lowering its cost of production.

A third factor is the practice group's expertise. Is the practice group readily seen by clients and competitors as among the best? Or are they more in the "journeyman" category – not that there's anything wrong with being a journeyman. Most of a corporate client's work is low- and mid-level and doesn't need the strongest and most expensive lawyers available. It's the old saying: For a particular type of legal work, do I need a Cadillac or a Chevy?

A fourth factor is competition and price elasticity. How saturated is the market with good, competitive lawyers at other firms, and what does that mean for pricing?

As already discussed, a final factor is balancing how much premium but episodic work a practice group wants and can get, versus the more routine but also much more sustainable (on a daily basis) work?

Practice groups will also differ internally. Each may have a very different method of working. Ironically, for some groups, it may make sense to have mostly partners, and yet law firm policies often reject such a concept. That is, for many/most practices, expertise may be far more important in creating client satisfaction as well as profitability when compared to the number of bodies that can be deployed. Yet most firms have artificial rules about how many partners any given practice group can have vis-à-vis other timekeepers.

Similarly, different practice groups have widely different needs for space and support services. The traditional formula of allocating overhead based on someone's rank (one and a half times salary for partners, one times salary for associates, and half of salary for paralegals) may significantly distort the amount of space and support services that are actually needed by any given practice group. For example, a particular practice group at my former law firm left to start their own firm. They reduced their rates and made more money at their newly created law firm. Our allocation of overhead, among other things, was distorting how profitable they actually were.

As previously noted, once practice groups are liberated from rigid formulas and allowed to make rational decisions for their particular specialties, it is usually quite remarkable the breakthroughs they can achieve. Their focus (finally) is how to significantly enhance the quality of their specialty, even if that means reducing rates, going to fixed pricing, using knowledge management and project management, and functioning with a larger portion of the team as partners.

How to set price

Factors that determine pricing include what is a competitive price for a task or matter in a given geographic market or industry, how much profit is desired, how to generate an outstanding product at a continually reduced cost of production, how to exceed client expectations, and how to get rewarded for results.

That requires looking at a firm's own data for past matters and tasks, and then considering how to significantly reduce the cost of production while still delivering an outstanding legal service. It also means looking at data that are increasingly available from third parties – including the average cost of matters and tasks in any geographic location or for any specific industry along with extensive details about specific law firms, practice groups, and even individual lawyers.

What this means for profitability and compensation

What all of this leads to is a need for law firms to differentiate their practice groups much more carefully. Among other things, this means having very capable practice group chairs or co-chairs, and then largely getting out of their way. Let them decide how to build cohesive relationships among the professionals that comprise the practice group. It also means the practice groups need to have considerable autonomy on how to price their work, and how to compete for that work. That in turn means compensation may vary widely between and within practice groups.

One possibility for computing profitability is first to measure the cost of production. That means totaling salaries and benefits for associates, paralegals, and support personnel; have a base number as a proxy for core partner income (the compensation-for-work part of partner compensation, versus the return-on-equity component); and add an allocation for space, central services, and other overhead.

One can then measure actual revenue received by practice groups, using some fair but not overly complex system for allocating revenue from matters that involve a number of practice groups, or lawyers who work in several practice groups. Practice group profitability then is actual money received (not billings in the pipeline), minus the cost of production.

One can then allocate some percentage of each practice group's profits (50 percent? 80 percent?) to members of the group, with the remaining percentage to be shared firm-wide. This allocation needs to be established at a point that will incentivize the practice groups to continually improve their profitability, and to see the results of those efforts, while still avoiding the syndrome that the firm becomes nothing more than a collection of silos.

Institutional values are very important, and thus some significant percentage of a partner's compensation (and even associate bonuses) needs to be based on the firm's overall performance. Among other things, the allocation of a firm-wide share of profits needs to help promote cooperation among the lawyers and practice groups and reward good firm citizenship (mentoring, serving on committees, and all the other activities that are important for a professional services organization).

That means the allocation to partners of points or other ownership percentages might be made by individual practice groups, but alternatively it might be better if a firm-wide process were to be used, employing firm-wide values. Whichever way points or similar ownership shares are allocated, ultimate partner income will be a combination of profits by practice group and profits of the firm overall.

Conclusion

Law firms and their leaders need to get away from the concept of top-down management, other than instilling core values and assuring basic quality standards. Rather, the firm should be seen as a collection of very different products and services since that, in fact, is how clients see the firm as well. Firms need to let each practice group have much more control over how they produce their particular legal services, sharing best practices with other practice groups, but not being required to slavishly replicate what everyone else does. Members of the practice group need to have readily understood incentives to focus on quality and profitability, and to be rewarded for their efforts. That needs to be combined with a commitment to the firm as an institution, and thus a stake in the firm's overall reputation and a share in the firm's overall profitability.

Chapter 8:
Four challenges in managing law firm profitability

By Jim Hassett, founder of LegalBizDev

When I conducted confidential in-depth interviews with managing partners, chairs, and senior executives from 50 AmLaw 200 firms for my book *Client Value and Law Firm Profitability*,[1] I was surprised by the magnitude of the differences of opinion about how to manage profitability, and the wide range of tactics firms use.

The problems are grounded in controversy over the very definition of law firm profits, and my book explains six key issues:

1. Relying on intuition;
2. Relying on revenue;
3. Focusing on profits per equity partner;
4. The varieties of realization;
5. The problem with leverage; and
6. Problems applying cost accounting.

These problems led directly to the four major challenges in managing profitability described in this chapter:

1. Lawyers' lack of understanding of profitability;
2. Controlling the bidding process;
3. Drawing the line between acceptable and unacceptable losses; and
4. Problems defining and rewarding profitability.

#1 Lawyers' lack of understanding of profitability

Given that law firms disagree about the best way to measure profitability, and that until a few years ago very few lawyers needed to worry about it, it is not surprising that understanding is limited at the individual lawyer level.

About half of the people I interviewed (26) were willing to provide a numerical estimate of understanding, when they answered this question: "How well do lawyers at your firm understand which matters and client relationships are profitable and which are not, from 1 (not at all) to 10 (very well)?" The average answer was a disappointing 4.8, with 2 as the lowest answer and 7.5 as the highest.

Senior executives at two firms expressed frustration with this lack of understanding:

> *Lawyers don't understand what profitability means or how they can influence that number. So it's a case of sometimes being focused on revenue, but not necessarily the right revenue, because they don't understand the profit trade-off. They say they've got an account that's giving two million dollars a year. Well that's fine. But if you're getting a three percent profit margin, stay in bed.*

> *We're still struggling with trying to communicate to our billing attorneys that when you agree to a 10 percent discount or a 20 percent discount, you've probably given away 100 percent of your margin. They don't get that. They say, "It's only a 10 percent discount."*

The biggest problem is in the area of discounting, since so many clients are requesting or requiring discounts these days, and so few lawyers understand the mathematical implications. In his book *Smarter Pricing, Smarter Profit*, Stuart Dodds proposes one simplified way of looking at this, which he calls the 1-3-4 Rule™:

> *For every one percent improvement in price, the potential increase to profitability is three percent. To get the same level of improvement in profitability without increasing price, you would need to work four percent more billable time.*[2]

Dodds goes on to explain that these numbers are an approximation, and that the precise relationship depends on the firm's margin. He even provides a table showing exactly how discounts from 1 percent to 20 percent reduce margin for firms whose margin before discount ranged from 20 percent to 50 percent.[3]

But for many lawyers, even the simple 1-3-4 Rule™ is probably too much math. Fortunately, in some firms lawyers have started to get the message, as described by this managing partner:

I would say we've got people that don't understand it at all, like a 1, and we've got some who understand it very well, like a 10. Probably, if you averaged all that out, we'd be 6 trending towards 7. We've come a long way, but we still have a long way to go.

#2 Controlling the bidding process

Given that many firms have established processes for getting approval on formal bids, it is not surprising that the numerical estimates went up a bit. When I asked "How well does your firm determine when the bid required to win a particular piece of business is too low and that it would be better not to bid, from 1 (very poorly) to 10 (very well)?" the average rating was 6.1. Not exactly impressive, but better than the 4.8 observed with individual lawyers. In this case, the lowest rating was 2 and the highest was 10.

As one senior partner explained:

Approvals are the first step toward better accountability. If you want to go well off the pricing norms, you need a series of approvals, and in the process of that, there's a fair amount of education going on about what can and can't be tolerated. So people are getting the message.

Others offered similar comments:

In our firm, there is an approval process for alternative fees. Now, is it done all the time? No. But it definitely helps that there are people who are looking at this. – Senior partner

I think our ability to make that determination is probably at the 8 to 9 level, with the caveat that assumes that we have an opportunity to make the assessment. But we certainly find from time to time that lawyers will get into an engagement where it turns out client expectations were different than they expected, or they didn't fully understand the parameters, and we have to do some scrambling to try and deal with it. – Chair

The best designed approval process in the world will not work if the initial scoping is done poorly. And bidding smarter means bidding at a reasonable price, even when it might lose, or sometimes not bidding at all, as seen in these comments from a senior executive and a chair at two different firms:

We've got a central approval process that includes all discounts, all alternative fees, all kinds of non-standard fee arrangements. We try to be very consistent across the globe to all of our clients, to make sure that we're equitable across the board. So when procurement sends out a big RFP, doing a rate survey and asking how big the discount is, we will always bid, but we'll bid what we give our largest clients, and nothing better. And so a lot of times, we don't win. If a client comes to us on a particular matter and says, "I can get it up the street for 100K," but we think it's going to cost 600K, then we will walk away, refuse to bid.

There are certain RFPs that I will not allow the firm to participate in. One is online auctions. Just won't do it. Another is when the whole focus seems to be from the procurement people, and the whole thing centers around price. Not quality, not who are your best litigators, not how do you plan to handle a case, what your success rate is. It's only driven by price.

Average ratings tend to go down when a firm gives more power to individual partners:

We have a fairly decentralized process at work. I spent this entire morning talking about our policies and procedures for approving deeply discounted and alternative fee arrangements. We discussed whether we should make changes and if we have the right system for our culture. We give a great deal of autonomy to individual partners. We don't like too much process and bristle at bureaucracy. As a result, in some cases we're a 1 and in some cases we're a 10, because we have avoided having a pricing committee. – Senior executive

Several participants pointed to the role of supply and demand in their bidding, like these senior partners from two different firms:

There are many times where we know it's too low and we bid anyway. There can be lots of good reasons. Beauty is in the eye of the beholder, and also, too low is in the eye of the beholder. The pressure to bid low is really significant, and we do that oftentimes with our eyes open. There are a few occasions where we say we're just not bidding, but it's rare.

Bidding is one of my pet peeves. I would churlishly rate us at a 1, but that's probably not fair. We have a reduced demand for services.

There is a lot of excess capacity, especially in general practice firms like mine, that are striving to find our place in a shrinking market. Some of our practice groups are out there competing with really efficient regional firms, with a very different cost structure than we have. In an individual case, for a particular piece of business, we don't say no often. It is rare for us not to bid at all. There are plenty of lawyers at large firms who just want to get busy. And so the only question they ask is, "What price would the client be willing to pay?" And general practice firms have a crisis of confidence. Too many times, the lawyers think, "Oh gosh, our rate is so high, and I don't know why they would pick me, and there are other people who are cheaper, so I will just race to the bottom."

#3 Drawing the line between acceptable and unacceptable losses

The world would be a simpler place if every single matter and every single case was expected to be profitable. At some firms, that goal may indeed be the best business strategy. But the larger the firm, the more likely it is that the best business strategy will require the firm to identify some losses on particular matters as acceptable if they can lead to higher overall profits for the firm.

As one survey participant noted in a follow-up interview:

Not every lawyer and every matter needs to be a profit center. Our firm has decided that we need to take some risks to grow market share in the current environment. We therefore distinguish between losses on a matter we took with eyes open to build market share and those that were mismanaged.

It is important to note that the business decision about which losses are acceptable and which are not are often based upon projections for the future, which may turn out to be correct or incorrect, and therefore can be the basis for lively debate. The most common rationales for "acceptable" losses are:

- To get some income for lawyers who have too little billable work;
- To meet all the needs of large clients;
- As part of a portfolio of cases; and
- To attract new clients.

Each of these rationales is discussed below. In our research, the reason mentioned most often for considering certain losses as acceptable is that firms have too much supply and not enough demand.[4] Consider these comments from six different firms:

It's kind of like an airplane. An empty seat gives you no revenue. So when we're evaluating bids or contingent fee cases, we look at the actual and predicted work load of the people who expect to be working on a matter. And we may make a different business decision if someone's well is pretty dry. – Managing partner

Sometimes we know a matter is not going to be profitable, but we take it anyway because we've got overcapacity that we're not going to be able to get rid of quickly. It's not profitable, but it's more profitable than zero. – Managing partner

We're in a situation right now where we have a lot of capacity, and we know it, but it's difficult to adjust in the short run. And so we consciously bid on items where we're not really covering all of our fixed costs. But we know that. If we could reduce capacity in the short run, then we would do that. But we can't. – Senior executive

Lawyers will look at a case or a client and say, "I know you don't want to get 70 percent realization on a $200,000 matter, but 70 percent of $200,000 is a lot better than 100 percent of nothing." – Chair

Sometimes we've said, "Listen, we don't want to lose these people, and I don't see anything else for them to do for the next three months." So when you look at profit margins, this might have been a negative 10 percent, but having them do nothing would have raised the cost of everybody else's matter, because I had the lawyers on the payroll whether they did any work or not. – Senior executive

Our pricing committee provides a level of sanity-filtering to all our proposals. For some proposals we just make the determination that we probably aren't going to make that much money on it, but at this point, we're not at capacity. That's the mindset within our pricing committee, anyhow. At the end of the day, very few opportunities are rejected. – Senior executive

Some believe that there are occasions when loss leaders are good for long-term business, like the senior partner who told us:

There are occasions when, all things considered, low pricing makes sense. It is an investment in cultivating and ultimately maintaining a relationship with a client over time, or in developing deeper experience in an area.

One anonymous reviewer gave this example:

We do ongoing patent prosecution that is not very profitable, but doing it lets us form a relationship with the chief patent counsel and impress the client with our patent expertise in ways that often lead to patent litigation engagements.

In a post-survey interview, one participant described a situation in which they had a very profitable relationship with a client for their M&A activity. To protect the relationship, they felt that they had to take on some unprofitable "commodity work" in another area. The irony of this case was that they applied LPM to the commodity work, changed the way they delivered the service, and ultimately the "commodity" work became more profitable than the M&A activity.

Still another reviewer of an earlier draft of this report noted that:

Firm management and consultants cleverly put something in a box called commodity work and then, having put it in this pejorative box, try to discard it. But commodity work can help pay for firm management and other overhead. It in fact may be far more profitable that the higher priced work, especially if the producers are paid appropriately.

A third reason for a loss being acceptable is as part of a portfolio of cases. As some clients increasingly look to have firms handle all of their cases in a particular area for a firm fixed price, losses may also be acceptable as part of a portfolio. As I wrote in my book *Legal Project Management, Pricing, and Alternative Fee Arrangements*:

One way to reduce the risk of a fixed fee is to handle many of them, so that there will be winners to balance out the losers. In stock portfolios, diversification helps to mitigate risk. With a wide selection of stocks, excess losses from a few unexpected losers can be offset by excess gains

> *from a few unexpected big winners. The principle of diversification is a key component of modern portfolio theory in finance. The same principle can be applied to a group of legal matters.*[5]

A fourth rationale for an acceptable loss is that a "loss leader" may get a foot in the door to develop new clients. Our research participants were far more skeptical about this concept than about the other three possibilities:

> *Lawyers don't think they're delusional when they say that they're going to lose money on the first deal but make it up in volume. Lawyers are prone to thinking that they can constrain profit a little bit on deal one, if they get, say, five deals… but lots of clients don't behave that way. So what happens is that the lawyer is making less money on this deal, but then the client gives the next deal to the guy across the street.* – Senior partner

> *Hope springs eternal. Some lawyers think that if they let this project expand a little bit, they'll produce a great result for the client, and the client will give them a bonus. And there are enough stories that are consistent with that belief that it's not entirely irrational for lawyers to sometimes think that way. The guy down the hall did get a bonus once, and my neighbor won the lottery.* – Senior partner

> *As one consultant told me a long time ago, there is no such thing as a loss leader, meaning, we can get our foot in the door. I liked to tell the lawyers that if you started buying your suits at Filene's Basement, and the quality was okay, it's going to be hard for you to pay $250, $300 more from Nordstrom's, and certainly it's going to be much harder to go to a custom tailor.* – Senior executive

> *I had one situation this week where I told the partner that I'm not authorized to approve loss leaders, that he needed to take that to someone else. And his pitch was that this is the first in what he thinks is going to be a long line of cases and this is what it's going to take to get our foot in the door. My response was, you get your foot in the door, and maybe you'll get all those other cases. But you've now created the expectation as to how much you're going to charge for them.* – Senior partner

While the debate may continue for some time about possible long-term benefits from loss leaders, there can be no doubt that clients are learning they can get high quality work delivered at costs so low that consultant Bruce MacEwen has coined the term "suicide pricing" for bids far below cost.[6] As long as there is a single firm that takes this approach, it will be hard for some clients to resist these low prices and for other firms to compete.

The challenge for every firm is to come up with a business model that meets client needs while protecting acceptable levels of revenue to compensate people fairly, and properly communicating firm strategy as explained in the next section.

#4 Problems defining and rewarding profitability

If law firms want to maintain and increase profitability, surely it would help if the lawyers who make deals knew how profitable their own work was and were paid more when their work was profitable. However, given the uncertainties over the best way to define profitability many firms feel that open communication is risky, as seen in these comments:

> *We have developed a tool that we use to measure profitability of individual engagements and of clients. There's some internal debate over whether that tool is as precise and accurate as everybody would like. We're using it, but we're being careful because we want to avoid an all-out competitive war among the lawyers in the firm in a way that might break up our teamwork.* – Chair

> *I think if we gave all the lawyers all of the data, we would just have a never-ending compensation conversation.* – Chair

> *We're trying to be careful with our profitability data, because people will say, "Can you tell me exactly how profitable my clients are?" The answer is no, because there are so many factors we can't measure. But we want to sensitize people to the fact that a million dollars from one client may not be the same as a million dollars from another.* – Managing partner

Law firms have very different philosophies about the transparency of both profitability and compensation. At one extreme:

There are no secrets. Everybody knows what everybody else is making. Total transparency. – Senior executive

At the other extreme, access to profitability information is very limited:

Redwood is our profitability module. We primarily use it in the back office to understand what's going on, so that we can be better informed, for example, when additional resources for a practice or for a client are requested, or to assist in the pricing of a particular practice. We've not really rolled this out to lawyers, because a lot of arguable assumptions obviously go into the underlying mechanics of Redwood. – Senior executive

The result at many firms is that lawyers know little about how profitability is measured at their own firms, including even some of the leaders we interviewed for this research:

We're now using something called Redwood, which I have not studied. There are two parts to Redwood, I guess. There's the stuff that our accounting people love, which they're using. On the project management side, I think someone else at the firm may have tried it. That software has not entered my life. – Senior partner

Where profitability information is shared it is often done in a controlled way:

We've just started going through it by client, calling in the billing attorneys as well as management, and trying to figure out where we can achieve improvement in a way that isn't overly destabilizing. – Chair

We don't embarrass our attorneys. If a shareholder is struggling, the people who see those results are their practice group leaders, department heads, and other shareholders in the group, since they're all owners. The intention is to encourage positive behavior rather than defensive. – Senior executive

Every partner has a year-end meeting with me as managing partner, where I communicate the results. They see the results in a published list, but at the meeting I communicate the thought-process of the compensation committee. And if there is a material problem with

their profitability, it's discussed. For example, we have some partners who do sophisticated loan work for national lenders and they get the documents out the door primarily with a partner and paralegal team. We have others who use a partner and a junior partner, or a partner and senior associate. So they're not equally profitable. To date, we've created opportunities for people to learn from each other and held up one as a good example and one as an example that needs improvement. We haven't really whacked anybody yet, but we're on the path to making it matter. – Managing partner

Several other firms also mentioned that the information is gradually becoming more visible within the firm, like this chair:

We're embarking this year on a broader dissemination. In the past we kept it pretty close to senior management, meaning me, and on occasion to practice group leaders or other people on our executive committee. We are reluctant, as I think a lot of firms have been, to share this information. Judging by people I've spoken to at a conference this summer, some firms have a much more forthright culture in discussing this, and others are in the middle. We're a very nice group of people and we're not so institutionalized as to shove it in people's faces or make them "get with the program or else." But I think we're overcoming some of our gentility and will start shoving it in people's faces a bit more.

When people were directly asked "Does profitability affect compensation?" 92 percent said "somewhat." The remainder were evenly split between "very much" (4 percent) and "not at all" (4 percent).

Several said things like:

We're still a subjective firm when it comes to compensation, so there's a whole host of factors that make up a person's compensation. – Managing partner

Others noted that:

The contribution to profit metrics has always been in what we call the comp book. It's a spiral-bound book of over 30 metrics that the comp committee looks at. So that's nothing new.... Any partner who wants to see it can get it. We have not widely disseminated the tool that specifically

measures matter profitability, because we want to really be careful that we don't encourage the wrong kind of partner behavior. – Chair

We don't have a formula system. Compensation is more subjective to begin with. Over the past couple of years, we've had more of a realization that profitability numbers really do mean something. And the accounting programs that we are looking at bringing in now are going to have a much more updated profitability system, so that everybody can understand that these are real numbers and they will be used. Not as the sole guideline or anything, and not as part of a formula, but as a factor in compensation. – Senior partner

We have a compensation committee that looks at many factors, including profitability. In some instances, someone's income is higher or lower than it otherwise might have been as a result of his or her profitability. But we wouldn't be able to say that someone made $50,000 or $20,000 less because of their profitability being where it is. – Senior partner

We don't pay people based on pure profitability, because so many things affect that, but if one person is more profitable on managing their matters than another, that's going to be a factor considered by the compensation committee. In other words, we don't say this person's increased profitability equates to $27,312 of more compensation, but we will compare relative profitability. – Managing partner

How should law firms adjust their compensation systems to protect their competitive positions and change lawyers' behavior? In my opinion, that is the single hardest question that law firms will face as they evolve to meet the changing demands of the marketplace. In many firms, annual debates over compensation were already a major management challenge even in the good old days when every year there was more money to go around. If the rules are changed at a time when many people are worried about their pay, it's not going to be pretty.

So exactly how should compensation be changed? There is no single answer, but at many firms compensation committees and consultants are actively working on the issue. As Tom Clay of Altman Weil summed it up in an interview:

For the last several decades, about 87 percent of law firm partner compensation has been based on originations and personal fee receipts, and 13 percent on a variety of other factors. Compensation systems must be carefully redesigned one firm at a time to reward the behaviors that will enable each firm to remain competitive in its marketplace, including finding ways to bring profitability into the equation to protect their margins.

References

1. Jim Hassett, *Client Value and Law Firm Profitability* (LegalBizDev, 2014).
2. Stuart Dodds, *Smarter Pricing, Smarter Profit* (ABA Book Publishing, 2014), 36.
3. ibid, 37.
4. If law schools have anything to do with it, the gap between supply and demand will only get worse. Law faculty members are protecting their own jobs by churning out more lawyers at a time when there are not enough jobs for them. As Steven J. Harper noted in *The Lawyer Bubble* (Basic Books, 2013, xii), "Nine months after graduation, only about half of the class of 2011 had secured long-term full-time work requiring a legal degree." Since then, there has been some reduction in law school applicants, "but the absolute number of applicants—sixty-eight thousand a year when the total number of new full-time jobs requiring a legal degree is twenty-five thousand a year and falling—remained absurdly high" (xv).
5. Jim Hassett, *Legal Project Management, Pricing, and Alternative Fee Arrangements* (LegalBizDev, 2013), 106.
6. Bruce MacEwen, *Growth Is Dead: Now What? Law Firms on the Brink* (Kindle edition, 2012).

Chapter 9:

Profitability, the concept of Managing on the Edge™, and their importance to a regional law firm

By James G Perkins, chief operating officer at Procopio, Cory, Hargreaves and Savitch, LLP

Introduction

In this article I introduce a basic primer on what I term "micro-profitability", the ability to measure and compare, with a reasonable degree of accuracy, such indicators as the profit of clients, matters, working attorneys, billing attorneys, practice teams, practice groups, and alternative fee arrangements. I also discuss how our matter profitability program is part of a management concept we have implemented, called Managing on the Edge™, to ensure our firm maintains a strong financial and profitable profile.

Reviewing the many articles written over the last few years on profitability one easily ascertains that the landscape is littered with warnings to tread warily. Quoting from different past articles; "a managing partner pointed out the underlying problem that there's really more art than science as to what you count as revenue and similarly what the cost allocations are going to be"; and from a another managing partner – "I've never heard of a law firm that has a good way to measure matter profitability. Many say they do, but when you push on the details it becomes clear that they really don't". One quote that goes to the heart of the issue; "the subject of profitability at the client and matter level is one that is very difficult to grasp for those not fully versed in cost accounting concepts. Whatever methodology is used, it should be agreed to by a consensus of the partners so that the results are accepted once the methodology is applied, and make certain that everyone buys into how the process is going to be done, and more importantly, why it is being done and what decisions will be made from the information once the analysis is completed." And from a senior manager of a profitability software product; "if I asked fifty law firms how they are measuring and using matter profitability I would get fifty different answers".

In the "fifty law firms" example however, each firm would likely agree with the importance of measuring profitability to improve firm management. If we asked them; "is your firm taking on clients and matters that are the bad for the bottom line", and a firm answered "no", then I think we would all agree that they are either in denial or the only firm in the world that is so "perfect". There is definitely a move afoot among leading law firms to change the dialog from the traditional "hours and revenue" to "revenue and profit". We think we are one of those firms.

Managing on the Edge™

In an article I wrote in the 1996 entitled "The Business of Running a Law Firm", and soon after I had become chief operating officer (COO) of Procopio, I made the statement that such comments by consultants as "lawyers did not know how to run a business" were nonsense. Law firms, managed and run by lawyers, had been making a profit for a long time and, as I saw it, the key factor was that competition in the legal market was weak and as such it did not require sophisticated business acumen to manage law firms and do well financially. Culture and tradition was the name of the game and regardless of whether the law firm's market was local, regional, or national (there were not many global firms back then) the ability to be financially strong was not that difficult. Matters were priced in an effort to simply get the work done without any real need to develop an understanding of the true cost of the engagement to the firm or its impact on profitability. The vast majority of firms had mastered what I term the "macro-approach" to profitability, the RULES[1] game, and could produce a solid firm profit at the end of the year. This situation continued for the vast majority of law firms up until the 2008 "crash". Given the changes that have occurred since 2008 and the many changes in the legal industry being forecast for the future, and as firms continue to adapt to an emerging procurement and alternative fee arrangement (AFA) environment in which clients increasingly expect their law firms to shoulder more risk in their engagements, law firm management has to now become a lot smarter if our firms are to survive and be sustainable in the long-term. It is critical that law firms develop the metrics to quantify both the revenue and costs at the client and matter level. Law firms will need to focus more on client and matter profitability, the "micro-approach" versus for example, realization percentages.

Our firm, like many regional firms in the country, plans to stay independent and as such needs to hold its own in the battle for talent against its main competitors – who are not only strong and innovative California firms, but also national and global firms. We need to be able to hire the best talent and compensate them such they are not tempted to move to our competition. This especially applies to our equity partners, who are the main rainmakers of the firm. We have to date been very successful in this endeavor in the main because several years ago we embraced a management philosophy we term Managing on the Edge™. As stated above, and like most successful firms, we have mastered the overall profitability of firm management that comes with understanding RULES, however to ensure revenue and profits are sustainable and grow year-over-year Managing on the Edge™ makes us focus on those activities "on the margin" that bring small positive incremental changes. These incremental changes, when added together, can make a substantial difference to the "bottom line". These incremental activities are mostly economic and directly affect the financials of the firm, for example a one percent increase in revenue, an "incremental" change, can result in a three to five percent increase in the net income. Such activities have included use of software to track all client "touches" in a day whether a document, a telephone call, or via an e-mail; use of automatically generated e-mails that contact clients when their invoices reach forty-five days past due; electronically generated paperless invoice proformas viewable anywhere in the world at any time on our virtual desktop system; a laser-like focus on improving standard to matter realization rates; reducing write-downs; and being smarter at AFA implementation. Other activities, like allowing clients a secure window into our business intelligence data or our collaborations with the Ritz Carlton Leadership Center to improve client service, have an indirect but long-term effect on our bottom line. Our recent focus on client and matter profitability, the "micro" approach to profitability, is the latest and potentially our most important Managing on the Edge™ incremental activity.

The macro-approach to profitability

Before we discuss the micro-approach to profitability, it is useful to say a few words about the historical macro-approach. The RULES approach for professional service firms appeared in the early '90's in the accounting world and was soon adopted by the law firm consultants. It has become the easiest way to focus on the management of law firm finances and profit. The "R" in RULES stands for realization, which is the percentage of work ultimately collected compared to the value of the work actually performed either at standard rates or at matter rates. A myth is that realization is the same as profitability, which is not true and can be very misleading if believed. Realization has been used incorrectly as a surrogate for profitability over the years, but as our own five years' analysis of the 15 percent of clients who give us 80 percent of our revenues shows, the correlation between realization and profitability, while a rough indicator, is not high. The "U" in RULES refers to utilization. The principle of utilization is to ask the question "how busy are you?" The firm has to set its standard for "full capacity". The "L" refers to leverage, which is simply the ratio of the number of lawyers who are not equity partners to the number of equity partners. Usually the calculation is based on the annual full time equivalent (FTE) number of partners and attorneys. The "E" in RULES refers to expenses and expense control, and the "S" serves as reminder that "speed of collections" is critical. When it comes to expense control, we are believers in "zero-based budgeting" techniques, a process that takes place at our firm every year. We assume no operating expense should continue year to year without being solidly vetted. Expense control also means that the firm should have a very solid understanding of the concept of fixed and variable costs and the differences between fixed/variable and direct/indirect costs. This understanding is essential to move from the macro-approach to the micro-approach of profitability.

Over the last twenty years or so, successful firms have learned to balance and manage the above RULES factors such that they maintained an acceptable level of profit (revenue less expenses). Other traditional financial indicators for law firms are revenue per lawyer (RPL) and profits per equity partner (PPEP) and, as shown in Figure 1, these two numbers can usually give a good indicator of a firm's ability to optimize all the RULES above. PPEP divided by RPL, called the Profitability Index (PI) should be equal to or greater than 1.0 (what I term the Magic Number). In many of the firms I have consulted with over the years, one of my first reviews is to determine their PI number, and if it is well below 1.0 then I know there is certainly room for major improvement in their profitability!

The micro approach to profitability

When one moves into the world of matter profitability one is entering into the world of cost accounting. The field of accounting has generally been divided into main parts, (1) financial accounting, and (2) managerial (cost) accounting. Financial accounting is primarily concerned with how accounting can serve *external* decision makers, banks, creditors, auditors etc., while managerial accounting is concerned primarily

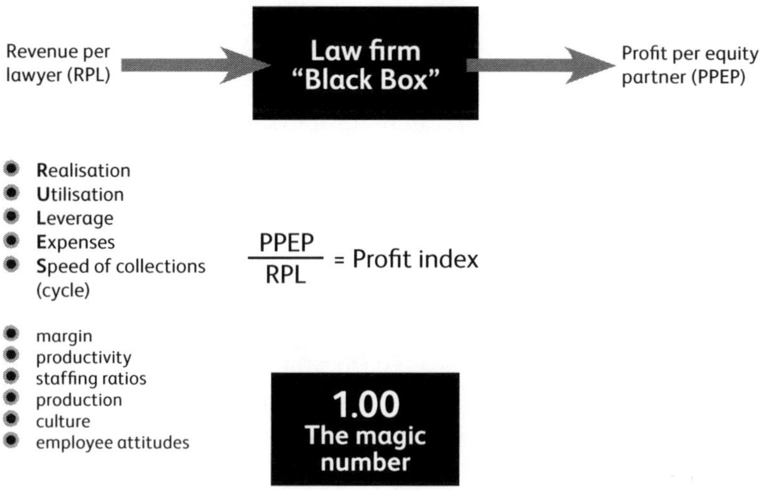

Profit index is the firm's ability to convert dollars coming in the door to dollars in partners' pockets

Figure 1: The law firm managerial accounting "Black Box"

with how accounting can serve *internal* decision makers, like the firm's management. This distinction is important because while there are "rules" for both types of accounting the internal ones are very flexible and allow more interpretation and assumptions, assumptions that are often decided by the management of the firm. Cost accounting is generally indistinguishable from so-called management accounting, or managerial accounting, and its fundamental aim is to assist management to make better decisions across a wide range of business operations. Thus law firm matter profitability needs to be understood in the context of the two very important drivers above: (i) it uses assumptions that are often decided by the management of the firm; and (ii) the aim is to assist management to make better decisions about firm operations.

Costs (expenses) are usually classified as either fixed and variable, or direct and indirect. While costs can be put into more than just two categories, it is sensible to focus on these two groups, as we can usually explain all that we need to with just these categories. Definitions of fixed and variable costs can vary from firm to firm, industry to industry, but for our internal purposes we classify fixed costs as ones that cannot be changed easily, if at all, in less than 12 months, whereas variable costs can be increased or decreased in a shorter period of time. Another way to view the difference is to say that costs that remain unchanged for a given time period despite wide fluctuations in activity are fixed, costs that change in proportion to changes in activity are variable. Examples of fixed costs in a law firm are rent, equipment leases, capital expenditures, and depreciation. Examples of variable costs are salaries, travel costs, and entertainment expenses. Fixed costs plus variable costs equal total costs, and revenue less total costs equal profit. Thus one can deduce that revenue less variable costs, what accountants often call contribution, is equal to fixed costs plus profit. When revenue exceeds variable costs, we have a positive contribution which first goes to cover fixed expenses and then it *contributes* to profit. This simple equation shows the importance of revenue, in that after it has covered all variable costs it first goes to cover fixed costs before any profit can be made. As law firm consultants all rush us to embrace matter profitability and profits, we must remember that revenue comes before profit, and revenue is extremely important and must not be forgotten. A client with a large revenue stream but with a lower profitability than the firm normal has an important role to play in the overall financial stability of the firm.

In professional service firms, just like other industries, there are also direct and indirect costs. Direct costs are usually always associated with variable costs and indirect costs to some form of overhead calculation or burden. However it is not true to say that all indirect costs are fixed or all direct costs are variable, as it depends on the costing model used by the law firm. In the macro model of law firm profitability it is usual to think of total costs rather than unit costs. Thinking in terms of unit costs however is required in a more granular analysis of profitability. In all cost accounting, regardless of what industry or profession is involved, unit costs are averages and must be interpreted cautiously. This cannot be emphasized enough. Analysis at the matter level of profitability is essential for firm management to understand the dynamics of cash flow and operations so that sensible ongoing business decisions can be made, however interpretation of the data developed can be misleading if the basics of the unit cost formulae are not understood. Different cost objectives can be used as units, for differing purposes, all of which can be very valid. Generally, unit costs are expressed in terms most meaningful to the people who are responsible for incurring the costs. In law firms or other professional partnerships acceptance of the overall unit cost model must occur with the shareholders/equity partners if the decisions that emanate from the model are to be implemented successfully. The partners must be "aligned" and accepting of the business model. The usual cost units that are cited in law firm profitability models and the ones that make most sense are (i) the individual, the lawyer; and (ii) the billable hour.

Problems start with how to estimate the cost of each hour of a lawyer's time, especially for an equity partner/shareholder's time. If a rainmaking partner is paid $1 million annually, how much of that was his or her direct cost for actually working on legal matters versus origination fees, payment for time spent on management, profit distribution, and other factors? Firms have tried a number of different systems of "notional compensation" to attempt to split compensation (and thus an important direct cost) between the amount allocated to billable activity and the amount for rainmaking and everything else. While not easy, a working attorney direct cost per hour must be calculated for equity partners/shareholders if a matter profitability model is to make sense. Even calculating associates (or other predominately non-rainmaking lawyers) direct costs is not easy. For example, suppose two-mid level associates in the same practice team earn the same $180,000 annual salary, but Associate A has 1,800 billable hours and Associate B has 1,500 billable hours. Assume all other benefits etc. are the same and for this simple example are ignored. Some firms might say that the direct cost of Associate A is $100 per hour ($180,000 / 1,800) while Associate B is more expensive at $120 per hour ($180,000 / 1,500). Now suppose the partners managing the relationship are rewarded on profitability, would they not try and assign work to Associate A rather than Associate B so as to increase matter profitability? And would not Associate A become even busier while Associate B gets further behind on billable hours? And so on, and so on until Associate A's direct cost becomes appreciably lower relative to Associate B and the overall system of allocating work sensibly and fairly to associates breaks down. The rule of unintended consequences looms large in the world of cost accounting for law firms.

Establishing a basic profitability model

Procopio uses profitability software by one of the leading law firm analytics service providers, DFTech. The first step in setting up a business model for profitability is to calculate for all timekeepers and staff the direct and indirect costs (overhead) that will be used in the model over the number of past years that the firm is planning to use in its calculations. We have defined costs from 2012 onwards. We also like using three year averages and three year data for much of our analysis, thus we now have in place costs for the 2012–2014 periods as well as for 2013–2015. By the end of January 2017 we will have the 2014–2016 data ready for review.

All timekeepers at Procopio are assigned to a specific practice team and each of those timekeepers have direct costs calculated from (i) their base compensation in the calendar year; (ii) their benefits paid in the calendar year; (iii) any bonuses paid in the calendar year; and (iv) an allocation for their professional liability insurance premium. Depending on the individual, there might be some other direct costs but we do not allocate as direct costs to individuals travel expense, marketing expense, office costs due to size, etc. We believe doing detailed personal allocations to try and differentiate such direct costs can be destructive and demoralizing and in fact the amounts are relatively unimportant in relation to final costs. We do however account for all these costs in an overhead that is weighted slightly differently depending on timekeeper category. For example, partners have a different weighting to associates, paralegals, etc. As stated above we have never subscribed to the policy of allocating every expense item to individual lawyers, timekeepers. And because of our overall approach using "bands" (see below), where we are not trying to differentiate between very small percentage differences in profitability, we know that these smaller expense amounts make little difference in the "big picture".

Once the total direct cost per individual timekeeper has been determined we can calculate the direct cost per hour for each. Herein is one of the major business model assumptions that have to be made in profitability at the matter level. What is the denominator in the per hour calculation? Is it actual billable hours worked, a "standard" number of expected billable hours per lawyer category, total hours expected to be worked in the year? As most time tracking and billing systems in law firms are based on the billable hour we selected, as a standard measure, a fixed billable hours quota for each lawyer category. So for example our "standard cost" unit per associate timekeeper is calculated by taking their direct cost and dividing by 1,850 hours. For partners we use 1,700 hours. Thus we develop a standard cost business model. With the DFTech software we can also easily perform, at the push of a button, calculations using the actual billable hours per year per individual timekeeper. This allows us to easily look at the "variance" from standard for every timekeeper or client, however in our view this analysis has limited value due to some of the anomalies already described above and the subsequent unintended consequences.

Indirect costs are all other expenses and costs not included in the direct costs above. One should note that in our business model the indirect costs also include each lawyer's objective bonus portions that are due to originations or for acquiring new business. How one measures and uses the bonus or other base compensation due to a lawyer's "book of businesses" or "new client credits" is worthy of another chapter in this booklet, but suffice to say for now that we include it as an "other" aspect of overhead. These indirect costs are allocated among all FTE timekeepers; lawyers, patent agents, paralegals, etc. From studies of the uses of resources by the various timekeeper categories, we have developed weighting ratios specific to each category for allocating the indirect costs (overhead). Partners are weighted slightly more than associates and associates are weighted more than paralegals. Thus, just as with direct costs, we can calculate an indirect cost per hour for all timekeepers. The direct cost per hour and indirect cost per hour are then added together to produce the total cost per hour for each timekeepers in our profitability model. Obviously the same timekeeper will usually have different costs per hour in different years. The individual cost per hour is then applied to every hour, or part hour, worked by the individual on every matter so we can develop the total cost for every client, every billing attorney, and every working attorney in any time period.

The detail above is actually a small part of setting up the business model for profitability and if you choose to do this with a vendor who has a good profitability model they will be able to take you through the myriad of steps required. However what I want to get across to the reader is that even the above initial "simple steps" of calculating direct and indirect costs per hour involves many assumptions. Different firms could well make different assumptions and thus the adopted profitability models, while they will have the same general accounting underpinnings, could well have different absolute results when applied to the same data set. However they will all probably reveal the same "relative" comparisons. Those clients whose profitability are above the firm average will show up in that same position in all analyses, the most profitable billing partner will appear at the top of all the business models, even though the actual calculated profit and profit margin might differ from model to model. A good profitability model will lead to analysis that is agnostic with regard to any firm's specific business model. At Procopio we have tried several profitability business models to prove out this theory, and in all the differing models, the most profitable stay the most profitable and the least profitable stay the least profitable.

It should be noted that when the final assumptions and business model is set, the final firm "average-normal" profitability in dollars and the profit margin percentage will be different from the firm's actual financials as shown on the accountant's and firm's internal statements. However for the business model to be credible one must be able to reconcile how the business model "ties in" with the actual firm financials. In our business model, and I suspect many others, the main difference comes from (i) the variance of actual overall firm annual billable hours versus the annual standards used; (ii) the fact that the business model uses a direct cost for equity partners whereas the financial income statement of a partnership does not record the equity partners as an expense; and (iii) time period differences especially when one has to consider the accrual aspect of work-in-process (WIP) and accounts receivable.

Using the profitability model

A sophisticated profitability software product based on a viable and credible profitability business model that spans several years' history is a very powerful analytical tool, and in addition has produced results that have been very enlightening. The results have dispelled some of the myths among the partnership that this client, or that client, was/was not very profitable, that this partner or that partner did/did not have a very profitable portfolio of clients. The actual results did not always follow the assumptions! The analysis also revealed that we had very few unprofitable clients or partners, that is, with profits of less than zero dollars or profit margins at or below zero percent. What the analysis did show however were the clients and the partners who had profitability well below the firm average and also highlighted those who were well above the firm average. We also believe it is more sensible to look at the relative position of clients and partners than to try and use an absolute profit number. We have thus developed the concept of "banding" or "grouping" the data around a norm. For example we have used a simple "band" model with five "bands" for profit margin analysis as shown in Figure 2. Such a simple graph can show profitability versus the annual fee collections by client, by partner. This is just one approach we have taken and obviously firms can have as many different types of analysis. The key, however, is to always remember that profitability analysis does a very good job of showing the relative positions of clients and partners as opposed to the absolute numbers. Because a cost accounting model in professional services firm has many assumptions we must be careful in trying to interpret and differentiate between a 25.7 percent and a 27.5

percent profit margin, but rather focus on whether the client or partner is above or below the firm norm by, 5 percent, 10 percent, 20 percent, or more.

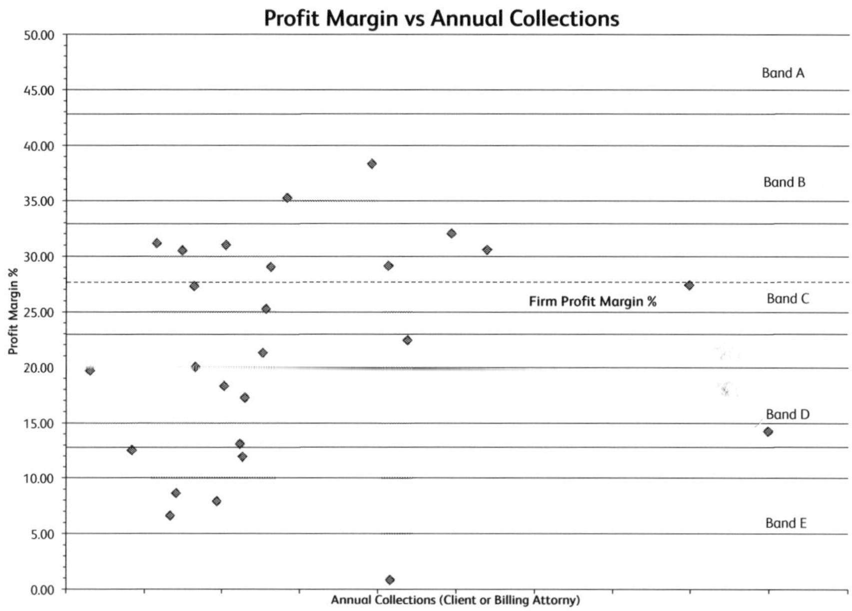

Figure 2. The "band" approach to using a profitability business model.

We have used the bands approach to compare the profitability by total dollars and by profit margin percentage for our practice teams, our clients, our attorneys as working attorneys and billing attorneys. We have done detailed profitability analysis on our various types of AFAs and the profitability of different groups of clients by their fees paid to Procopio. We also discovered that the overall profitability of clients in different revenue groupings is not that much different, and that the smaller revenue groups are as profitable as the larger ones. The ability to do sensitivity analysis on profitability, that is, change one or two parameters easily and see what effect the changes have on profitability, allows us to work with all attorneys on a one-on-one basis to improve the profitability of the clients they are responsible for, and to help them manage the mix of attorneys and other time-keepers they use on their client portfolio. This is especially important for those attorneys with the larger "books of business". It thus allows the partners to better manage their client portfolio and the non-partner and non-lawyer timekeeper staff that are under their control. We use the profit models and their results to help educate the attorneys on the "cost" of human resources, and it also helps them to budget more accurately on large litigation or transactional matters and to develop project scopes more efficiently. Knowing the historical profitability of clients when we open new matters for them will also help us develop more appropriate matter plans.

We have started to review how we will use our bands approach to profitability in compensation decisions. I suspect like all law firms that are grappling with the same issue we are treating it cautiously. While law firm consultants have preached for several years that compensation should contain an important profitability component,[3] and on the face of it that makes perfect sense, Procopio is probably like 99 percent of other law firms in that the key to compensation is revenue, not profitability.

Conclusion

We have no doubt that the implementation of a cost accounting profitability program at the matter level will allow us to continue to deliver quality legal services in an improved, efficient, cost effective, and profitable way. Profitability modeling is not a panacea and it does not substitute for great lawyers, solid policies and procedures, top-notch ethics, and all the good traditions of a top law firm. It is however a very important new component in our Managing on the Edge™ program that we hope will allow us to remain independent and super competitive with our regional, national, and global law firm friends. Hopefully it helps our ongoing efforts to keep our best talent and attracts others. So in conclusion a reminder of some key points from our experiences:

- Cost accounting is a very good "relative" comparison method, a not so good absolute measure;
- Unit costs used in cost accounting are mostly averages and must be interpreted cautiously;
- Be careful of timing issues. Measuring profitability has to be within a set time period so remember that you are trying to calculate the fees collected on the work done in that time period, so at the end of the time period both work-in-process and accounts receivable will probably play apart and have to be included. Also an accrual approach can be taken;

- If during the time period being reviewed the client(s) were new and growing then the profitability measured might not reflect correctly, especially if for some reason the client(s) have long work-in-process periods, as we experience in our patent prosecution work;
- The profitability business model(s) you use must be able to be reconciled back to your actual accounting financials in the time periods being considered; and
- Before jumping to make decisions with the profitability results make sure that whether you are considering clients or attorneys there are no extraneous factors at work, and if there are that you understand their effects.

And remember, the business model for micro-profitability should be decided by firm management, so don't be afraid to develop several different ones before deciding on the right one for your firm. Then make sure you align your partners with how the model works and how it is intended to be used, before you use the data for serious decision making. And a final word of caution. There are challenges present in measuring and managing "profit" in a law firm such that firm's management should explore how they best navigate their cultural landscape before plunging forward!

References

1. Fiebert G., *Mind Your Rules*, Smock Law Firm Consultants, 2014.
2. Ibid.
3. Altman Weil, *Linking Partner Compensation with Profitability*, Altman Weil Webinar, 2014.

Chapter 10:

Case study – Strategy and culture driving effective use of people, process, and technology at Faerge Baker Daniels

By Mark Voigtmann, Steve Petrie, Vanessa Savoie, and Tom Snavely of Faerge Baker Daniels

Background

At Faegre Baker Daniels, our firm culture is the driving force that guides us to work in an efficient manner and to enrich the client experience. Our "Clients First" service standard leads us to continuously ensure that we (i) use the right people, (ii) develop innovative processes, and (iii) deploy leading edge technology. These efforts are supported by the firm's pricing, legal process improvement, and legal project management programs which are now in their seventh year. On select matters, the firm first applies proven process-improvement methods to optimize staffing, workflow, and technology. We then tailor traditional project-management tools to meet the requirements of individual matters, thus ensuring efficient execution, and enhanced communication. As our efficiency programs evolve, we recognize that they are only sustainable if they are part of our firm-wide culture.

In practice

An example of how FaegreBD has leveraged pricing, legal process improvement, and project management originated from our construction practice. This practice used our comprehensive approach to expand its footprint within a niche market. The niche market in question involved companies in the business of integrating computers, software, and robots within industrial processes. After a decade of acting as general counsel for a trade association of 395 engineering firms engaged in this specialty (52 outside the US) and performing legal services for many of its members, the firm was uniquely positioned to serve this niche market. The association wished to offer a legal program to its members to expand its organizational attractiveness and vitality. The construction practice endeavored to leverage this existing relationship to enhance its exposure across this member organization, develop new client relationships, and bring in more complex work. Faegre Baker Daniels worked with association leadership and multiple internal departments to develop an innovative structure and approach that leverages our people, processes, and technologies in the efficient delivery of outstanding legal service.

Pricing

A menu-based proposal with loss leader "freebies" and "tickler" offerings plus various flat fee options was developed based on historical time entry data. An hourly discount was applied to our standard rates for litigation and other extra scope matters; however, these discounts were not so deep that they would be unsustainable. Among the freebies: members of the association are automatically enrolled in the legal program offering, each receiving a free 30-minute consultation as a benefit with time in excess of the initial consult billed at the discounted hourly rate. The association agreed to a one-year term so that the program can be adjusted if needed. The one-year period was crucial for minimizing firm exposure, as expected volume across 400 potential clients is difficult to predict.

Process improvement

After a pricing arrangement was reached, a cross-functional team was established to determine the best operational approach. The practice-group leader began by setting an objective that all front end tasks (many of which are typically handled by lawyers) would now be completed by paralegals or non-timekeepers and that lawyer time was to be conserved exclusively for legal work. The practice-group leader created a process map that identified who does what, when, and how. The map was reviewed with the legal and operational team members to improve the process by eliminating waste, leveraging technology, setting expectations, and building adoption.

Legal project management

Scope

It quickly became apparent, through the process improvement exercise, that achieving an accurate determination of scope prior to commencing legal work would be critical to the efficient use of people within the process. The lead attorney built a script that allows a "project coordinator" (non-attorney) to identify client needs and expectations prior to an attorney commencing legal work. The consistency of the scoping script resulted in a standard approach by which attorneys could efficiently engage with clients without excess administrative time.

Schedule

The expected volume of matters was daunting, and the legal team expressed a desire to ensure that "no client or matter would fall through the cracks." The firm's KM department developed a user-friendly, web-based dashboard to ensure that due dates, team expectations, and matter status are universally understood by the legal team.

Budget

As the matters were priced aggressively, and often on a fixed fee, tracking our actual time-value investment and comparing it regularly to the budget or fixed fee became increasingly important for profitability. The firm's Financial Systems department developed a set of email alerts that are sent automatically when a matter reaches predetermined financial milestones, as well as a weekly summary of all consortium matters in process. Email alerts allow the legal team to see the information quickly and conveniently.

Results

The firm's comprehensive approach allowed it to build a foundation for increased, profitable growth in this niche market. Initial results following the introduction of the program indicate moderate success with further opportunities for process improvement. The practice group gained new matters, new clients, and has achieved a healthy realization thus far, with only mixed success to date in the goal of removing attorneys entirely from the client intake process. In an effort to continually improve, administrative resources will be adjusted so that they are more aligned with the staffing model of the plan, and the team will look closely at the data to determine if tweaks to the menu pricing are eventually warranted.

Future

As we have evolved as an organization, we have begun to lay a foundation for continuous improvement, to ensure that we serve our clients through the best application of our people, processes and technologies. "Continuous improvement" is an organizational mindset, characterized by the tenacious pursuit of enhanced service that delights and exceeds the expectations of internal and external clients alike. The firm has sought to cultivate such a mindset by setting clear direction, empowering people, and encouraging creativity. A culture of continuous improvement enables our people to challenge the status quo by identifying new and better ways to complete their work. This has resulted in a more pervasive and enduring focus on proactive evaluation and improvement of the client experience. This is not accomplished overnight, but is an evolutionary byproduct of a series of small innovative steps/projects. Innovative thinking can serve our clients by delivering value, increasing efficiency, reducing costs, and differentiating our firm, and we will continue to develop and deploy our people, processes, and technologies in pursuit of those strategic ends.

Case study contributed by Tom Snavely, manager of legal process improvement and project management; Steve Petrie, chief strategy officer; Mark Voigtmann, partner; and Vanessa Savoie, senior strategic analyst and pricing analyst.